The Mandolin Picker's
to Bluegrass Improvisation

by Jesper Rübner-Petersen

Online Audio www.melbay.com/22086BCDEB

LCCN: 2010921507

1 2 3 4 5 6 7 8 9 0

Visit us on the Web at www.melbay.com — E-mail us at email@melbay.com

AUDIO CONTENTS

1 Quarter Notes (pg. 6)
2 Eighth Notes (pg. 6)
3 Quarter/Eighth-Note Example (pg. 7)
4 Slide Example (pg. 7)
5 Arpeggio Example (pg. 12)
6 Variation Example (pg. 13)
7 Bluegrass Arpeggio Style Example (pg. 14)
8 Double-Stop Shuffle Example (pg. 15)
9 Shuffles+Slides Example (pg. 15)
10 Double-Stop Shuffle+Licks Example #1 (pg. 16)
11 Double-Stop Shuffle+Licks Example #2 (pg. 16)
12 Licks Using Pentatonic Scales Example #1 (pg. 18)
13 Licks Using Pentatonic Scales Example #2 (pg. 19)
14 Licks Using Pentatonic Scales Example #3 (pg. 19)
15 Licks Using Pentatonic Scales Example #4 (pg. 19)
16 Licks Using Pentatonic Scales Example #5 (pg. 20)
17 Licks Using Pentatonic Scales Example #6 (pg. 20)
18 Licks Using Pentatonic Scales Example #7 (pg. 21)
19 Licks Using Pentatonic Scales Example #8 (pg. 21)
20 Licks Using Chord Progressions Example #1 (pg. 22)
21 Licks Using Chord Progressions Example #2 (pg. 22)
22 More Advanced Pentatonic Scales Example #1 (pg. 24)
23 More Advanced Pentatonic Scales Example #2 (pg. 24)
24 More Advanced Pentatonic Scales Example #3 (pg. 24)
25 More Advanced Pentatonic Scales Example #4 (pg. 25)
26 More Advanced Pentatonic Scales Example #5 (pg. 25)
27 More Advanced Pentatonic Scales Example #6 (pg. 26)
28 Slow Improvising Example #1 (pg. 26)
29 Slow Improvising Example #2 (pg. 27)
30 Slow Improvising Example #3 (pg. 27)
31 Slow Improvising Example #4 (pg. 28)
32 "Easy Playing" Improvisation Example #1 (pg. 30)
33 "Easy Playing" Improvisation Example #2 (pg. 32)
34 The Minor 3rd Example #1 (pg. 34)
35 The Minor 3rd Example #2 (pg. 34)
36 The Minor 3rd Example #3 (pg. 35)
37 The Minor 3rd Example #4 (pg. 35)
38 The Minor 7th Example #1 (pg. 36)
39 The Minor 7th Example #2 (pg. 36)
40 The Minor 7th Example #3 (pg. 37)
41 The Minor 7th Example #4 (pg. 37)
42 The Perfect 4th Example #1 (pg. 38)
43 The Perfect 4th Example #2 (pg. 38)
44 The Perfect 4th Example #3 (pg. 38)
45 The Major 7th Example #1 (pg. 39)
46 The Major 7th Example #2 (pg. 39)
47 The Major 7th Example #3 (pg. 40)
48 Connection Lines Example #1 (pg. 40)
49 Connection Lines Example #2 (pg. 41)
50 Connection Lines Example #3 (pg. 41)
51 Mixing the Ideas Solo #1 (pg. 41)
52 Mixing the Ideas Solo #2 (pg. 43)
53 Mixing the Ideas Solo #3 (pg. 44)
54 Mixing the Ideas Solo #4 (pg. 44)
55 One-Bar Licks Example #1 (pg. 46)
56 One-Bar Licks Example #2 (pg. 46)
57 "Last Line" Licks Example #1 (pg. 47)
58 "Last Line" Licks Example #2 (pg. 48)
59 "Last Line" Licks Example #3 (pg. 48)
60 "Last Line" Licks Example #4 (pg. 48)
61 "Last Line" Licks Example #5 (pg. 48)
62 "Last Line" Licks Example #6 (pg. 49)
63 "Last Line" Licks Example #7 (pg. 49)
64 "Last Line" Licks Example #8 (pg. 49)
65 "Last Line" Licks Example #9 (pg. 49)
66 "Last Line" Licks Example #10 (pg. 50)
67 "Last Line" Licks Example #11 (pg. 50)
68 "Last Line" Licks Example #12 (pg. 50)
69 The G Chord Example #1 (pg. 51)
70 The G Chord Example #2 (pg. 52)
71 The G Chord Example #3 (pg. 52)
72 The G Chord Example #4 (pg. 53)
73 The G Chord Example #5 (pg. 53)
74 The G Chord Example #6 (pg. 53)
75 The G Chord Example #7 (pg. 53)
76 The C Chord Example #1 (pg. 56)
77 The C Chord Solo #1 (pg. 56)
78 The C Chord Solo #2 (pg. 57)
79 The F Chord Solo #1 (pg. 59)
80 The F Chord Example #1 (pg. 60)
81 The F Chord Example #2 (pg. 60)
82 The F Chord Solo #2 (pg. 60)
83 The B♭ Chord Example #1 (pg. 63)
84 The B♭ Chord Example #2 (pg. 63)
85 The B Chord Example #1 (pg. 64)
86 The B Chord Example #2 (pg. 64)
87 The B Chord Solo #1 (pg. 66)
88 Double-Stop Licks Example #1 (pg. 68)
89 Double-Stop Licks Example #2 (pg. 69)
90 Double-Stop Licks Example #3 (pg. 69)
91 Double-Stop Licks Example #4 (pg. 70)
92 Slides Example #1 (pg. 72)
93 Slides Example #2 (pg. 73)
94 Mixing the Structures Solo #1 (pg. 73)
95 Mixing the Structures Solo #2 (pg. 74)
96 The Picked Slide (pg. 76)
97 Movement 1 (C-Major) Lick #1 (pg. 76)
98 Movement 1 (C-Major) Lick #2 (pg. 76)
99 Movement 1 (C-Major) Lick #3 (pg. 77)
100 Movement 1 (C-Major) Lick #4 (pg. 77)
101 Movement 1 (C-Major) Lick #5 (pg. 77)
102 Movement 1 (C-Major) Lick #6 (pg. 77)
103 Movement 1 (A-Major) Lick #7 (pg. 77)
104 Movement 1 (A-Major) Lick #8 (pg. 77)
105 Movement 1 (A-Major) Lick #8 (pg. 77)
106 Movement 1 (A-Major) Lick #10 (pg. 77)
107 Movement 1 (A-Major) Lick #11 (pg. 78)
108 Movement 1 (A-Major) Lick #12 (pg. 78)
109 Movement 1 (E-Major) Lick #13 (pg. 78)
110 Movement 1 (E-Major) Lick #14 (pg. 78)
111 Movement 1 (E-Major) Lick #15 (pg. 78)
112 Movement 1 (E-Major) Lick #16 (pg. 78)
113 Movement 1 (E-Major) Lick #17 (pg. 78)
114 Movement 1 (E-Major) Lick #18 (pg. 78)
115 Structure 1 (E-Major) (pg. 79)
116 Structure 2 (A-Major) (pg. 79)
117 Structure 3 (B-Major) (pg. 79)
118 "Playing Around with Double-Stops" Solo (pg. 79)
119 The Ghost Note (pg. 80)
120 Variations on the Picked Slide Example #1 (pg. 81)
121 Variations on the Picked Slide Example #2 (pg. 81)
122 Variations on the Picked Slide Example #3 (pg. 81)
123 Connecting the Structures Example #1 (pg. 83)
124 Connecting the Structures Example #2 (pg. 83)
125 Connecting the Structures Example #3 (pg. 83)
126 Connecting the Structures Example #1 (pg. 84)
127 Connecting the Structures Example #2 (pg. 84)
128 Connecting the Structures Example #3 (pg. 85)
129 Chord Tones Harmonized in 6ths (pg. 86)
130 The use of "Passing Double Stops" (pg. 87)
131 Major Scale Movement Lick #1 (pg. 87)
132 Major Scale Movement Lick #2 (pg. 87)
133 Major Scale Movement Lick #3 (pg. 88)
134 Major Scale Movement Lick #4 (pg. 88)
135 Major Scale Movement Lick #5 (pg. 88)
136 Major Scale Movement Lick #6 (pg. 88)
137 Major Scale Movement Lick #7 (pg. 89)
138 Major Scale Movement Lick #8 (pg. 89)
139 Major Scale Movement Lick #9 (pg. 89)
140 Major Scale Movement Lick #10 (pg. 89)
141 Major Scale Movement Lick #11 (pg. 90)
142 Major Scale Movement Lick #12 (pg. 90)
143 Major Scale Movement Solo #1 (pg. 90)
144 Scale Movement Played in 6ths (pg. 92)
145 Example 144 Played in 3rds (pg. 92)
146 Harmonizing in 3rds Solo #2 (pg. 93)
147 Chord-Related Movements Example #1 (pg. 94)
148 Chord-Related Movements Solo #3 (pg. 94)
149 The Minor 7th Sound Example #1 (pg. 95)
150 The Minor 7th Sound Example #2 (pg. 96)
151 The Minor 7th Sound Example #3 (pg. 96)
152 The Minor 7th Sound Example #4 (pg. 96)
153 The Minor 7th Sound Example #5 (pg. 97)
154 The Major 6th Sound Example #1 (pg. 97)
155 The Major 6th Sound Example #2 (pg. 97)
156 Double Stops Played with Tremolo (pg. 98)
157 The "Banjo Waltz Technique" (pg. 98)
158 Minor Chords Solo #1 (pg. 100)
159 Dorian Scale/Minor Scale Example #1 (pg. 102)
160 Dorian Scale/Minor Scale Example #2 (pg. 102)
161 A-minor (no 6th) Scale Example #1 (pg. 103)
162 A-minor (no 6th) Scale Example #2 (pg. 103)
163 A-minor (no 6th) Scale Solo #2 (pg. 104)
164 The (IIIm) Chord Solo #3 (pg. 105)
165 The (IIIm) Chord Solo #4 (pg. 106)
166 The (IVm) Chord Example #1 (pg. 107)
167 The (IVm) Chord Example #2 (pg. 107)
168 The (IVm) Chord Example #3 (pg. 107)
169 The (IVm) Chord Example #4 (pg. 107)
170 Horizontal Playing Example #1 (pg. 109)
171 Horizontal Playing Example #2 (pg. 109)
172 Horizontal Playing Example #3 (pg. 110)
173 Symmetrical Sequence #1 (pg. 110)
174 Symmetrical Sequence #2 (pg. 111)
175 Symmetrical Sequence #3 (pg. 111)
176 Symmetrical Sequence #4 (pg. 111)
177 Adjustable Playing Example #1 (pg. 112)
178 Adjustable Playing Example #2 (pg. 112)
179 Adjustable Playing Example #3 (pg. 113)
180 Adjustable Playing Example #4 (pg. 113)
181 The V Chord in a Minor Key Example #1 (pg. 114)
182 The V Chord in a Minor Key Example #2 (pg. 114)
183 The V Chord in a Minor Key Example #3 (pg. 115)
184 The V Chord in a Minor Key Example #4 (pg. 115)
185 The V Chord in a Minor Key Example #5 (pg. 115)
186 The V Chord in a Minor Key Example #6 (pg. 116)
187 The A-harmonic minor (no 6th) Scale (pg. 116)
188 The Blues Scale Blues Solo (pg. 118)
189 The Blues Scale Solo #1 (pg. 118)
190 The Blues Scale Solo #2 (pg. 119)
191 The Blues Scale Added the Major 3rd (pg. 120)
192 "Mountain Fever" (Major) (pg. 121)
193 "Mountain Fever" (minor) (pg. 121)
194 Blues Scale with Mountain Minor Tune Solo #3 (pg. 122)
195 Mountain Minor tune (non-bluesy) Solo #4 (pg. 123)
196 Extended Blues Scale Example #1 (pg. 124)
197 The Monroe Style Solo #1 (pg. 126)
198 The Monroe Style Solo #2 (pg. 126)
199 The Monroe Style Solo #3 (pg. 127)
200 The Monroe Style Solo #4 (pg. 127)
201 The Monroe Style Example #1 (pg. 128)
202 The Monroe Style Example #2 (pg. 128)
203 The Monroe Style Example #3 (pg. 129)
204 The Monroe Style Example #4 (pg. 129)
205 The ♭7 as Leading Tone Example #1 (pg. 129)
206 The ♭7 as Leading Tone Example #2 (pg. 130)
207 The ♭7 as Leading Tone Example #3 (pg. 130)
208 Mixing the Licks Solo #5 (pg. 130)
209 Two-String Crosspicking Example #1 (pg. 132)
210 Two-String Crosspicking Example #2 (pg. 132)
211 Two-String Crosspicking Example #3 (pg. 132)
212 Two-String Crosspicking Example #4 (pg. 133)
213 Slides Example #1 (pg. 133)
214 Other Groupings Example #1 (pg. 133)
215 Other Groupings Example #2 (pg. 134)
216 Other Groupings Example #3 (pg. 134)
217 Melodic Lines Example #1 (pg. 134)
218 Melodic Lines Example #2 (pg. 135)
219 Mixing the Ideas Example #1 (pg. 135)
220 Mixing the Ideas Example #2 (pg. 136)
221 Three String Crosspicking Example #1 (pg. 136)
222 Three String Crosspicking Example #2 (pg. 136)
223 Three String Crosspicking Example #3 (pg. 137)
224 Three String Crosspicking Example #4 (pg. 137)
225 Three String Crosspicking Example #5 (pg. 137)
226 "Will the Circle Be Unbroken" (Trad.) (pg. 141)
227 "Will the Circle Be Unbroken" Solo #1 (pg. 141)
228 "Will the Circle Be Unbroken" Solo #2 (pg. 142)
229 "White House Blues" (Trad.) (pg. 143)
230 "White House Blues" Solo (pg. 143)
231 "John Hardy" (Trad.) (pg. 145)
232 "John Hardy" Solo (pg. 146)
233 "Dark Hollow" (Trad.) (pg. 147)
234 "Dark Hollow" Solo (pg. 148)
235 "Wayfaring Stranger" (Trad.) (pg. 149)
236 "Wayfaring Stranger" Solo (pg. 150)
237 "Pretty Polly" (Trad.) (pg. 152)
238 "Pretty Polly" Solo #1 (pg. 153)
239 "Pretty Polly" Solo #2 (pg. 153)
240 The Major Scale Example #1 (pg. 155)
241 The Major Scale Example #2 (pg. 155)
242 Key Related Playing Example #1 (pg. 156)
243 Key Related Playing Example #2 (pg. 156)
244 The IV Chord Solo #1 (pg. 157)
245 The M7 and the Major Scale Sound #1 (pg. 158)
246 The Root→M7→6th Movement (pg. 158)
247 Neighbor Tones (pg. 160)
248 Chromatic: 3rd→5th Example #1 (pg. 161)
249 Chromatic: 3rd→5th Example #2 (pg. 161)
250 Chromatic: 3rd→5th Example #3 (pg. 161)
251 Chromatic: 3rd→5th Example #4 (pg. 161)
252 Chromatic: 3rd→5th Example #5 (pg. 162)
253 Chromatic: Root→ ♭7 (pg. 162)
254 Chromatic: Root→ 6th (pg. 162)
255 Chromatic: 2nd→3rd (pg. 163)
256 Mixed Chromatic Example #1 (pg. 163)
257 Mixed Chromatic Example #2 (pg. 163)
258 Minor Chords Example #1 (pg. 165)
259 Minor Chords Example #2 (pg. 165)
260 Improvising Using Substitution Example #1 (pg. 167)
261 Improvising Using Substitution Example #2 (pg. 167)
262 Improvising Using Substitution Example #3 (pg. 168)
263 Improvising Using Substitution Example #4 (pg. 168)
264 Where/How to Use Substitutions Example #1 (pg. 168)
265 Where/How to Use Substitutions Example #1 (pg. 168)
266 Playing Triplets Example #1 (pg. 170)
267 Playing Triplets Example #2 (pg. 170)
268 Mixing Ideas (pg. 171)
269 Large Movements Example #1 (pg. 171)
270 Large Movements Example #2 (pg. 171)
271 Rhythmic Displacement Example #1 (pg. 172)
272 Rhythmic Displacement Example #2 (pg. 172)
273 Rhythmic Displacement Example #3 (pg. 172)
274 Rhythmic Displacement Example #4 (pg. 173)
275 Rhythmic Displacement Example #5 (pg. 173)
276 Rhythmic Displacement Example #6 (pg. 173)
277 Rhythmic Displacement Example #7 (pg. 173)
278 Rhythmic Displacement Example #8 (pg. 173)
279 "Temperance Reel" (pg. 174)
280 "Temperance Reel"– Easy (pg. 175)
281 Skipping Tones Example #1 (pg. 177)
282 Staying on Chord Tones Example #1 (pg. 177)
283 Staying on Chord Tones Example #2 (pg. 177)
284 Solo #2 from Chapter 10 (pg. 178)
285 Limited Improvisation Example #1 (pg. 179)
286 Lick Replacement Example #1 (pg. 179)
287 Lick Replacement Example #2 (pg. 180)
288 Chord Progression #1 (pg. 200)
289 Chord Progression #2 (pg. 200)
290 Chord Progression #3 (pg. 200)
291 Chord Progression #4 (pg. 200)
292 Chord Progression #5 (pg. 200)

TABLE OF CONTENTS

About the Author/Credits 4

Introduction 5

Chapter 1   Theory 8
             The major scale (pg. 8)
             Intervals (pg. 10)

Chapter 2   Chord Tones 11

Chapter 3   For the Beginner 15
             The double-stop shuffle (pg. 15)

Chapter 4   The Pentatonic Sound 17
             The major pentatonic scale (pg. 17)

Chapter 5   Let's Play Bluegrass 23

Chapter 6   Slow Improvising 26

Chapter 7   Stationary Improvising 29

Chapter 8   Let's Improvise 30
             Troubleshooting (pg. 30)
             Easy playing (pg. 30)

Chapter 9   The Spices 34
             The minor 3rd (pg. 34)
             The minor 7th (pg. 36)
             The perfect 4th (pg. 37)
             The major 7th (pg. 39)
             Connection lines (pg. 40)

Chapter 10   Mixing the Ideas 42

Chapter 11   One-Bar Licks 45

Chapter 12   "Last Line" Licks 47

Chapter 13   The G Chord 50

Chapter 14   The C Chord 55

Chapter 15   The F Chord 58

Chapter 16   Other Major Chords 61
             The B♭ chord (pg. 61)
             The B chord (pg. 63)
             Transposing "up the neck" (pg. 64)

Chapter 17   Double-stops 67
             The structures (pg. 67)

Chapter 18   "Playing Around" with Double-stops 75
             The movements (pg. 75)
             The picked slide (pg. 76)
             Ghost notes (pg. 80)

Chapter 19   Other Double-Stops Ideas 82
             Connecting the structures (pg. 82)
             Other double-stops shapes (pg. 83)
             Chord numbers (pg. 85)
             Harmonizing the major-scale (pg. 85)

Major-scale movements (pg. 86)
Chord related movements (pg. 93)
The minor 7th sound (pg. 95)

Chapter 20   Minor Chords 99
             The dorian scale (pg. 99)
             The minor scale (pg. 100)
             The minor (no 6th) scale (pg. 102)
             The phrygian scale (pg. 104)
             The (IV m) chord (pg. 106)

Chapter 21   Minor Keys 108
             The minor scale (pg. 108)
             Horizontal playing (pg. 108)
             Symmetrical sequences (pg. 110)
             Adjustable playing (pg. 112)
             Vertical playing (pg. 113)
             The V chord in a minor key (pg. 113)
             The harmonic minor scale (pg. 114)
             The harmonic minor (no 6th) scale (pg. 116)

Chapter 22   The Blues Sound 117
             The blues scale (pg. 117)
             Mountain minor (pg. 120)
             The extended blues scale (pg. 123)

Chapter 23   Monroe Style 124
             "Anticipating the tonic" (pg. 128)
             The ♭7 as leading tone (pg. 129)
             Down strokes (pg. 131)

Chapter 24   Cross Picking 131
             The two-string cross picking technique (pg. 131)
             The three-string cross picking technique (pg. 136)

Chapter 25   The Melody 138

Chapter 26   Other Spices 154
             The major scale (pg. 154)
             The mixolydian scale (pg. 159)
             Neighbor tones (pg. 160)
             Chromatic (pg. 160)
             The minor-pentatonic scale (pg. 163)
             The relative minor (pg. 165)
             Chord substitutions (pg. 166)

Chapter 27   Hot Licks 170
             Triplets (pg. 170)
             Large movements (pg. 171)
             Rhythmic displacement (pg. 171)

Chapter 28   How to Simplify a Lick 174
             Skipping tones (pg. 174)
             Staying on chord tones (pg. 177)
             Limited improvisation (pg. 178)
             Lick replacement (pg. 179)

Conclusion   180

Appendix   181

ABOUT THE AUTHOR

Photo: www.ersted.dk

Hi mandolin-pickers! I'm Jesper Rübner-Petersen and I was born on the 8th of July 1969 in Aarhus/Denmark, where I grew up with Bluegrass and Acoustic Music because of my banjo-playing father. At the age of 12 I started to play the guitar and as soon as I was ready to grab a couple of chords I luckily got the chance to play in different Oldtime and Bluegrass Bands. Besides playing bluegrass, I've always tried to be open about new influences and decided to follow the jazz program at the "American Institute of Music" in Vienna, Austria, which I completed in March 1993. Staying at the A.I.M. opened up my eyes to harmony and theory and the understanding of improvisation. Around 1994, after years of intensive guitar playing, I bought myself a mandolin in order to try out a second instrument — a purchase which changed my life. In July 2000 the destiny of love made me move to South Germany, where I also started my professional career as a guitar and mandolin teacher. At the same time, I started teaching at Beppe Gambetta's Summer-Workshop, the International Workshop Musique Acoustique in Belgium, the Mandolin-Workshop at the New Acoustic Gallery and other local workshops. Over the years, while traveling around doing concerts and workshops, I often was asked questions about improvising and how to do it. After some research, I figured out that the demand of improvisation knowledge seemed to be international and so came the idea about writing an improvisation book to my mind.

CREDITS

- To write this book about bluegrass improvisation was a process that took me several years to finish. This project wouldn't have been feasible without the support and consent which I got from my lovely wife **Anna Rübner-Petersen**.

- Another huge acknowledgement goes to the American mandolin player **Spencer Sorenson** who spent quite an amount time proofreading the manuscript. – Thank you Spencer.

- I would also like to thank all the American bluegrass musicians who have toured around Europe, providing us with inspiration and a lot of good music.

- And of course I'd like to thank all the musicians from our local oldtime and bluegrass association, who inspired me as a young boy to go on with the music (especially **John Andersen**).

- Every note I play is done in the memory of my father **Jørn**, who taught me about bluegrass music. Thanks to my dear mom **Karen** and my cool brother **Morten**, but also to the rest of my lovely family in Denmark: **Helen, Lotte, Michael, Mads, Rosa** and **Asta**. Thank you **Edelgard** for being the best mother-in-law.

- A last thank you goes to all of my friends and fellow musicians and all of my mandolin students.

INTRODUCTION

What is improvisation:

Improvisation is, for the most part, a technique i·
often used by bluegrass musicians in jam sessi
tune. But improvisation is also a technique
Improvisation in its basic form does not
ture, using the chord progression as a

In order to be able to improvise
learn to improvise is a process in
about learning to improvise, is to ge
to do your first small, improvised solo. _
you're "infected" by the "improvisation viru

Where to use improvising:

As already stated, improvisation is a technique which o.
tunes. An improvised solo could also be used on a well-kn
But also if you would like to play a melody-based solo, it's rea.
rules and tools for making some new variations on the melody l.

Also banjo instrumentals are often used for improvising. To imitate a b.
difficult and probably also the reason that a lot of players use improvisatio.
tunes have a weaker melody line on the B part, which makes it obvious that a.
with active back-up (instrumental playing behind the lead singing vocal) it is cou.

Some musicians are so deeply into improvising that they'll take every opportunity they
fact that it's a challenge to play an improvised solo, might also make some players push the
provisations on some difficult chord changes. In some situations improvisation could also be a
fun– play something wild, but smile! The ultimate improvising situation might be the "duelin' im
and forth trying to raise the level by every new break. This is show-time and the audience likes it.

Improvisations have always had their part in bluegrass-based music, no matter if we're talking traditional c
grass, newgrass or new acoustic music. The spirit of the tune was and will always be the guideline for the imp.
the right kind of soloing (fast or slow playing, bluesy or not, single-note lines or double-stops, melody or harmo..
playing, etc.).

All though I'm a big fan of improvising, I won't the be the judge about when or how to use improvising. It's really up to
you to acquire a feeling for the situation.

How to use this book:

The ideal way to use this book might be one where the reader works his way through each chapter, one at a time. The logi-
cal way might be to read the whole book first, in order to get an overview and then to start from the beginning playing
the exercises and doing the assignments. The third way might be one where the more advanced mandolin player picks out
different chapters to work on, after reading the book once. How you work with this book really depends on you and your
playing skills.

Some of you might ask yourself: "How long does it takes to learn the material from the book?" – and my answer will be:
"Half a year, one year or several years." In fact, it doesn't matter. Everybody learns differently and so this book should also
be treated individually. The learning process won't work if it's rushed. Take your time. Use the book as a supplement to
other things what you are learning at the same time. The book could also be used as a reference book for the more advanced player. A teacher and his student could also work on exercises and assignments from this book, combined with the

teacher's own philosophies, solo analyses an
It's quite important to emphasize that thi
ideas related to specific famous mandoli
grass styles, in order to make the reade
from other points of view than that o
improvisation differently. As you lea
of other players on recordings. Try
in the book in their solos? If ther
what you have learned here. It's
figure out your own way of thin

Technique:

In order to get the right b
nique called alternate pi
into a system. By expla

Down-stroke =

The following exa
the notes, you'll
etc. Our first r
or beat four),

...l transcriptions, for example.

...s book is a method on how to learn to improvise. The book does not contain ...n players. I've tried to keep the material neutral to the different kinds of blue- ... come out with his own style. The theme of improvisation can surely be looked at ... this book. Every improviser has his own way of thinking and every teacher teaches ...n the method of improvisation presented, it is a very good idea to listen to the solos ...to understand how they go about playing the solos. Can your hear some of the ideas ...e is something you think that sounds good, try to play it, or something close to it, using ...quite a good idea to use this book along with any other influence you can get, in order to ...king– your philosophy.

...uegrass sound, while playing the examples in this book, I suggest that you use the picking tech-...king. Alternate picking is a technique where the order of the played down- and up-strokes are put ...ning the system, I'll use the following symbols for the down- and the up-strokes:

Up-stroke = V

...mple will show us a measure in which four quarter notes are played. By counting the beats while playing ...ee that every one of the notes is played on a beat. The first note on beat one, the second note on beat two, ...le could now be formulated like this: Every note which is played on a beat (beat one, beat two, beat three ...hould be played with a down-stroke.

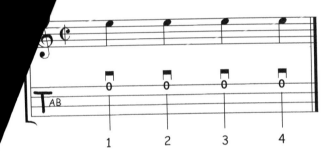

The next example will now show us how the eighth notes should be played and counted. As you can see, we'll play all notes coming on the "ands" (the off-beats) using up-strokes. So, the second rule will be: Every note which is played on the off-beat should be played with an up-stroke.

 # 2

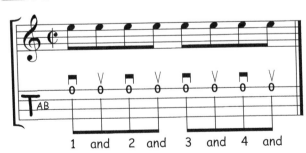

In order to be able to play lines mixing up quarter and eighth notes, using the right down- and up-strokes, I've written down a couple of exercises to play. At the very end, the exercises might be kind of tricky to play. But don't worry, most of the examples in the book use simple rhythms and shouldn't cause you any big problems.

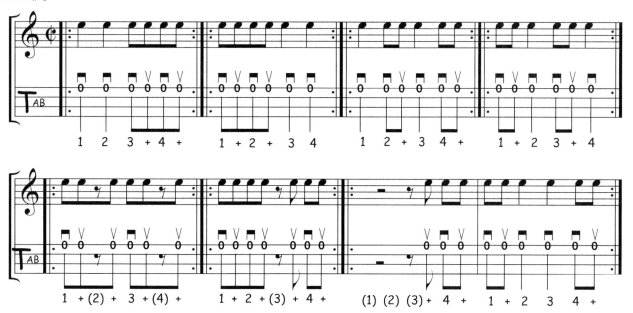

One last problem when playing alternate picking might be how to treat a lick containing slides. When playing a slide, we're kind of skipping one stroke with the right hand. This might cause you some problems if you're not used to slides. A stroke in the air (written like this (⊓) or (∨)) while doing the slide, might also be a big help for some of you.

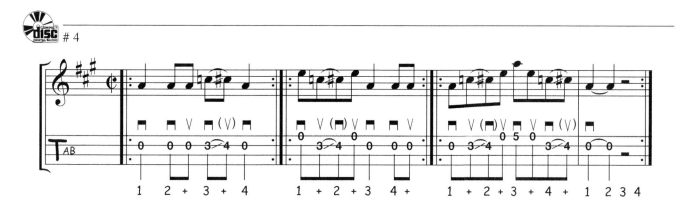

The fact that the down-strokes are accented more strongly than the up-strokes is one of the reasons that alternate picking automatically provides us with the right bluegrass sound. Beyond giving us the right accents to the music, alternate picking also brings us the right flow.

If you've never heard about alternate picking before, it might take you some time to get it into your playing. Learning alternate picking is like learning to swim– when it's learned, you'll never forget it again and it comes automatically. Alternate picking is certainly the most common picking technique in bluegrass music, but towards the end of this book a couple of other picking techniques will also be covered (See Chapter 23 and 24 - Monroe style and cross-picking).

Fingerings:

The fact that a lot of mandolin players have had fiddle or guitar as their first instrument, influences the fingering they use while playing the mandolin. Fiddle players seem to use the pinky in spots where guitar players would prefer to change positions, or a guitar player might use the pinky on a line where a fiddle player would prefer to stretch his fingers. I did add some fingerings to a couple of the examples in the book (see the standard notation), but basically it's up to you to figure out how to make the fingerings as comfortable as possible. Don't hesitate to try out different fingerings in order to find ones that fit you the best.

Before starting to read the book:

Before you set out on your journey into the world of improvising, I'd like to thank you for buying this book. I really hope it will bring you some interesting time (by learning and by doing). And don't forget! – Take your time and have fun!

Keep on improvising!

Jesper Rübner-Petersen

CHAPTER 1: Theory

In this first chapter I've chosen to start out with the theme of theory. Music theory is a way of explaining what's going on in music. It's a very big subject covering the names of the scales, the structure of the chords, the intervals between the notes and many other interesting things. For an improviser it's quite important to know something about the theory. The theory also supplies us with a "music-language" to use when explaining musical subjects or for example improvising techniques.

In order to keep everything simple, I've picked out the most important basics of theory for this chapter. As we then move along with the other chapters in the book, our knowledge about the theory will be extended. You'll actually learn the theory by playing the examples and exercises.

The major scale:

The most important scale in music theory is the major scale. It's a scale containing seven notes played one after each other in series. Play the following A-major scale and listen to its sound. The last note is the same as the first, but played one octave higher.

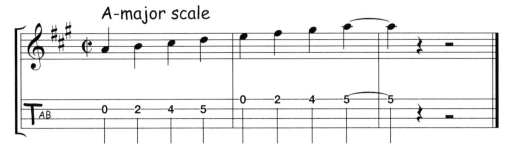

If we play the A-major scale on one string only, it's easy to see that the scale is built of whole and half-tone steps. The distance between one note and another note played two frets higher is a whole-tone step. The distance between one note and another note played one fret higher is a half-tone step. As you can see, I've written down the whole- and half-tone steps on the following A-major scale.

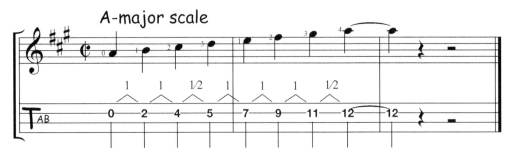

The very first note in the scale is called the root. The root is the note that gives the scale its name. In the major scale shown, the root would be the note a and the scale would be called the A-major scale. If a major scale starts on the note d, for example, the root would be the d note and the name of the scale would be the D-major scale.

8

The interval between the root and the second note in the major scale is called a major 2nd interval. The interval between the root and the third note in the major scale is called a major 3rd interval. The remaining intervals are:

The root – the fourth note: perfect 4th interval
The root – the fifth note: perfect 5th interval
The root – the sixth note: major 6th interval
The root – the seventh note: major 7th interval
The root – the eight note: octave interval

Not only does the first note of the major scale (the root) have a name. The other notes of the scale are named after the intervals. In this way, the second note of the major scale is also called the major 2nd (because of the major 2nd interval between the root and the note).

The third note is called: the major 3rd
The fourth note is called: the perfect 4th
The fifth note is called: the perfect 5th
The sixth note is called: the major 6th
The seventh note is called: the major 7th
The eighth note is called: the octave (root)

Take a look at the A-major scale and the names of the notes.

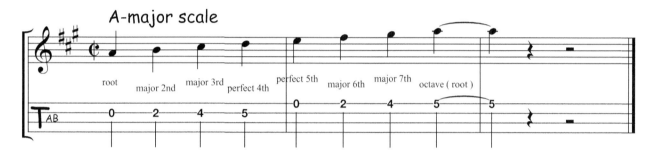

The notes in between the notes from the major scale also have names.

The note a half-tone below the major 2nd, is called: the minor 2nd
The note a half-tone below the major 3rd, is called: the minor 3rd
The note a half-tone below the perfect 5th, is called: the diminished 5th
The note a half-tone below the major 6th, is called: the minor 6th
The note a half-tone below the major 7th, is called: the minor 7th

As you already might have guessed, these five (in between) notes are all named after the intervals too. This way, the interval between the root and "the minor 3rd note" is also a minor 3rd interval etc.

Check out this example, in which all twelve notes are written out with their names.

Intervals:

As we already learned, the distance between the root and the major 2nd is called a major 2nd interval or a whole-tone step (two frets). The note a half-tone step above the root, would be the minor 2nd (one fret). In the following example, the steps between the root and the intervals we have just learned are all written out, in order to understand the intervals better.

Until now, the root was used as the starting point for building intervals. But in fact, it's possible to use every tone on the mandolin as a starting point for building intervals. To demonstrate this, I've written out a couple of examples in which different tones are used for building intervals.

Minor 3rd intervals

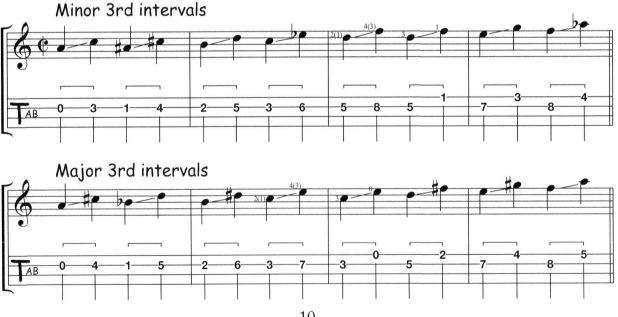

Major 3rd intervals

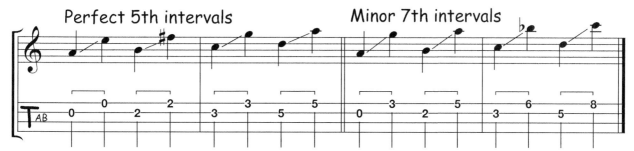

In order to simplify the theory, I won't go into details about why some intervals come as minors and majors and other not (for example, the perfect 4th). To explain this now would be too comprehensive and might even make things more confusing. For now, we just need to know to names of the intervals. But if you like to know more about this subject, it's recommended that you read some books about harmony and theory. It will explain everything and it's even quite interesting.

The major pentatonic scale:

Another important scale is the major pentatonic scale. As you probably already know, penta means five and the pentatonic scale actually is a scale containing five notes. The structure of this scale is quite simple. Just take the major scale, but leave out the perfect 4th and the major 7th, as in the following examples

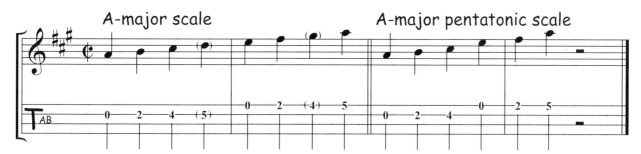

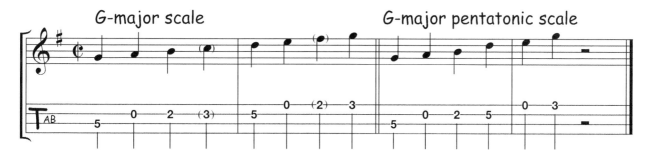

In the appendix you'll find an overview of all major and pentatonic scales.

CHAPTER 2: Chord Tones

The structure of a major chord is very easy to explain, now that we know the structure of the major scale. To build a major chord, we need to take the root, the major 3rd and the perfect 5th from the major scale, as done in these examples:

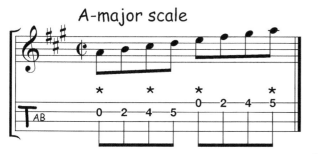

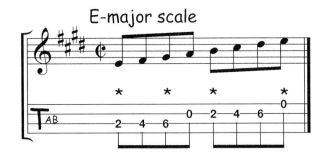

E-major scale

E-major arpeggio

If we play these three tones at the same time, we have a major chord. When we play an A-major chord on the mandolin, for example, the chord will contain the tones: a, c♯ and e. Because of the "four" strings on the mandolin, one of the tones appears twice (often the root). As an exercise, try to figure out what notes a D-major chord contains (in the appendix you can find the D-major scale, if you don't know it already).

Three chord tones played in a row make up what is called an arpeggio. Arpeggios can also be used as an improvising tool. In the following example, I'll show you how it could be done. On the A-major chord I play a small A-major arpeggio motive/lick. On the D- and the E-major chords, I do the same thing with a D- and a E-major arpeggio.

5

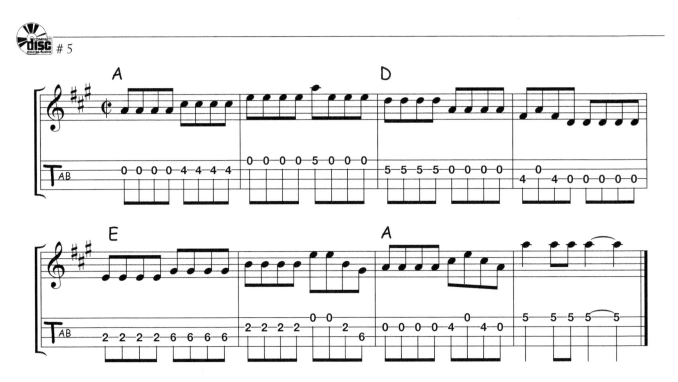

When we use arpeggios as an improvising tool, it's important to know the arpeggios by heart. In order to make an improvisation sound more melodic, we need to be able to play our arpeggios on at least the three highest strings. Our extended arpeggios would sound like this:

A-major arpeggio

D-major arpeggio

E-major arpeggio

A small exercise would be to do some variations on the next example. As you can see, it's not necessary to start on the root all the time. If you let the last tone ring for half a bar, it would give you a little time to get to the nearest tone of the following arpeggio. After playing the example a couple of times, it's time for you to come up with some variations starting on other chord tones. Be sure you know the arpeggios by heart before doing the variations.

6

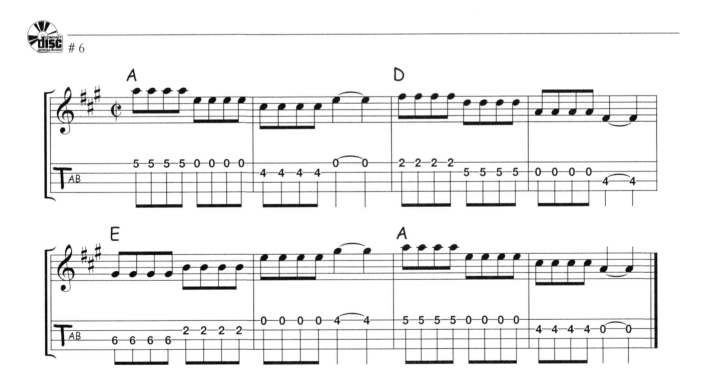

Check out the next example in which a common "bluegrass arpeggio style" is demonstrated.

13

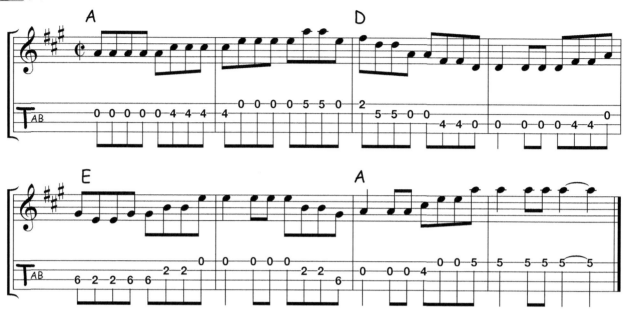

Minor chords:

If you need an arpeggio for a minor chord, you must use the following structure:

Root → minor 3rd → perfect 5th

In this last example the difference between the major and the minor arpeggio is shown. As you can hear, it's the 3rd that gives the arpeggio its special character.

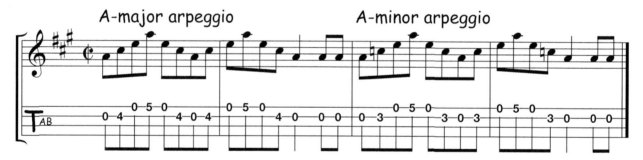

Notice:

In the following chapters all chords will be written like this:

For example. (A-major chord) = A chord
Or (A-minor chord) = Am chord

The major pentatonic scale will also just be referred to as the *pentatonic scale.*

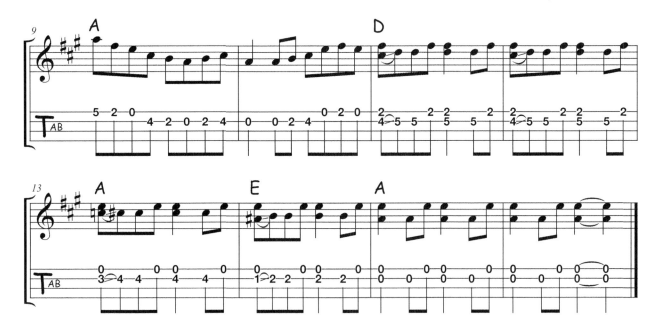

As you can see, we only used the scale-related licks on the A chord. This way of mixing up licks with "double-stop shuffles" can be really helpful if you would like to simplify some of the upcoming examples and exercises. Also when composing solos (see Chapter 6: Slow Improvising) or when you have to improvise in real time, the "double-stop shuffles" technique could be effectively used.

Another technique which might help you in the following chapters, is the "let's skip some notes" technique. This technique will be covered in Chapter 28 (How to Simplify a Lick).

CHAPTER 4: The Pentatonic Sound

This might be the most important chapter in the entire book. This is because not only will we make the first steps into the "world of improvising," but also because we'll learn the foundation of bluegrass improvisation - the pentatonic scales.

If you have read the first chapter about theory, you already know that a pentatonic scale contains five different notes. Now let's take a look at the first three pentatonic scales. The very first one is the A-pentatonic scale, which fits the A-major chord. The next is the D-pentatonic scale, belonging to the D-major chord and at last the E-pentatonic scale which could be played over the E-major chord. At first, they might not sound particularly "bluegrassy," but they will later on! Trust me!

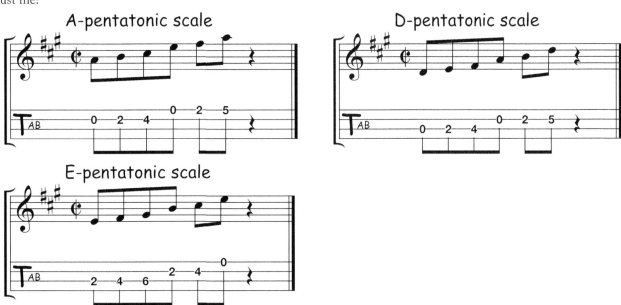

In the following example we have the same pentatonic scales written out in a box system, showing the neck of the mandolin and the played frets. This way of writing out the scales in a box system helps you to visualize the shapes of the pentatonic scales better (the appendix explains how to read the box system).

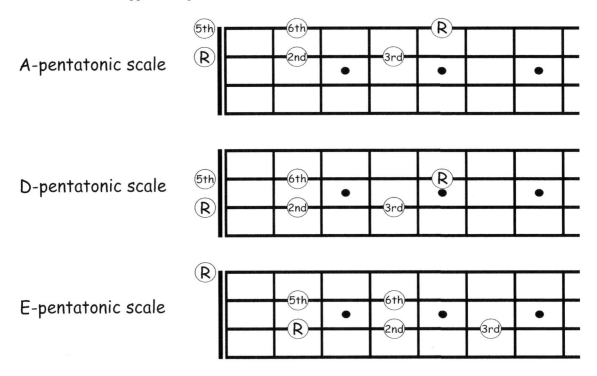

A-pentatonic scale

D-pentatonic scale

E-pentatonic scale

Like crossing a river by walking on big stones, we can also pick the notes in these shapes without getting "wet feet." Said another way: Playing pentatonic licks on the right chord, nearly can't go wrong. So let's get started!

I've written out some licks using the pentatonic scales. The fact that I'm only using one octave scale and always transposing the licks from one chord to another, might give the exercise a slightly mechanical sound. But the main goal right now is to learn these scales, picture them in your mind and become familiar with them. It's important to learn improvisation one step at a time. So play the next examples over and over again and get used to the sound of the pentatonic scales. Playing over the E chord might not seem so easy, but don't worry, in a later chapter you'll learn some new tools that will help. On the last A chord in the line, I might play a non-transposed lick, in order to make the ending sound more smooth.

12

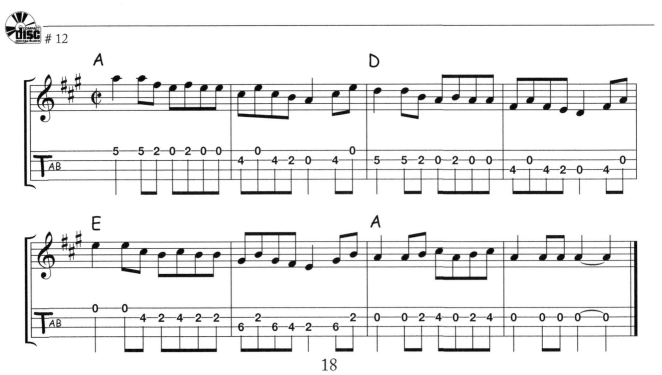

13

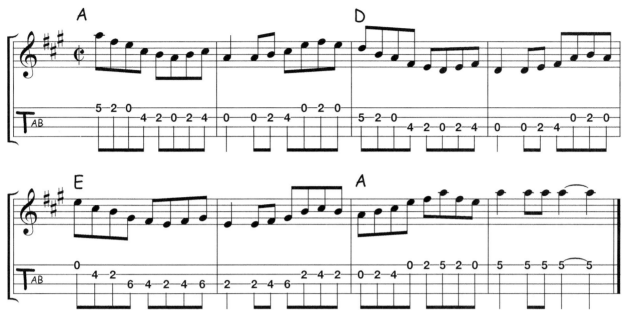

 # 14

 # 15

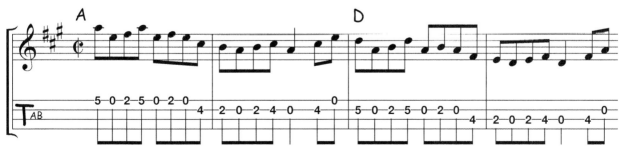

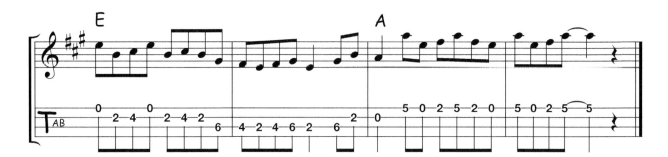

As you might have noticed, the licks just played all started on the root tone of the chord. But a lick could also be started on the major 3rd or on the perfect 5th of the scales, as you can see in the following example. To make the endings of the lines sound more correct, I chose to start on the root of the last A chord.

18

19

From now on, I'll give you some assignments to do at the end of each chapter. These assignments are extremely important and I highly recommend that you do them. But don't get stressed out now. Take your time. Find a quiet place where you can "study" undisturbed. Take your mandolin, some standard notation or tablature paper, a pen and let's get started.

ASSIGNMENTS

1.   Write out a two-bar pentatonic lick, using the one octave A-pentatonic scale. Don't make it too difficult. The lick should be playable and easily learned.

2.   Transpose the lick to D by moving the A lick one string lower.

3.   Now transpose the lick to E, which isn't so easily done. Every note in the D lick should be played a whole tone higher (two frets).

4. Play the licks together in a row as we did in the exercises. If it doesn't work, you might have composed a lick that is too difficult. If this is the case, then recompose your lick and make it work.

If you have never tried writing out something in music notation/tablature, it might not be the easiest thing to do. The most common problem is to write out the right rhythm of the composed lick. Don't worry! – For now, just write the notes in the lick without the rhythm. If you can play your lick, it's good enough for me. The more you play the examples in this book, the better you'll start to understand the length of the notes and how to write them.

Another problem that might appear is the fact that not all lick changes sound good. If the interval between the last played note in a lick and the first of the following lick is too big, it might sound strange. But, don't forget, we are still learning and it doesn't have to sound 100 percent perfect yet.

Let's continue with the assignments.

5. Until now we have only used the chord progression **I A I A I D I D I E I E I A I A I**. Try to play your own composed licks in a different order using this chord progression:

These last two examples will show you how the licks we have learned can fit another chord progression.

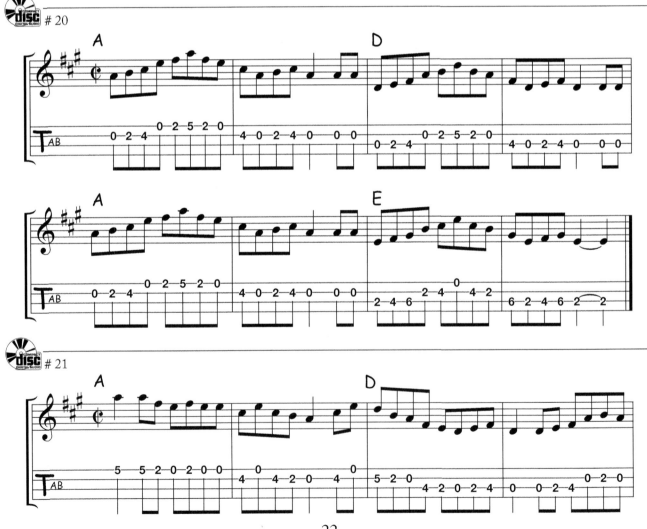

22

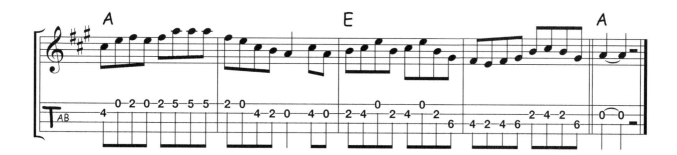

CHAPTER 5: Let's Play Bluegrass

The purpose of "one octave scales" are to simplify the learning and the picturing of those scales. So, if you can play the material in the previous chapters, you are on the right track. If you can't play all three pentatonic scales and some pentatonic licks by heart, I highly recommend that you work some more on the assignments in the last chapters.

Up until this point the exercises didn't really sound like a common bluegrass solo. The examples were quite limited in their use of notes and were more intended for the purpose of learning. To go a step further, we'll extend our "one octave pentatonic scales," as you can see in the next three box systems. The added notes are all notes belonging to the pentatonic scales we know, but played an octave lower or higher.

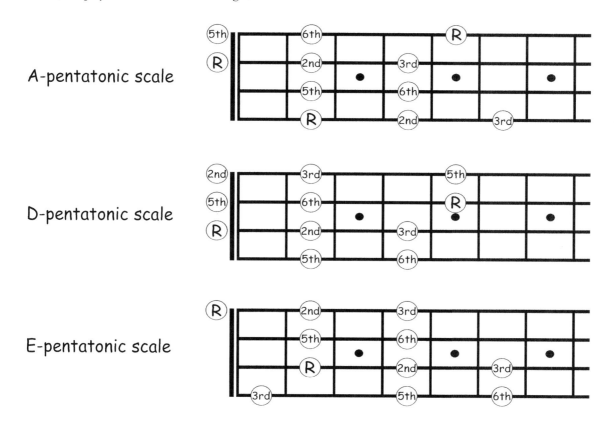

A-pentatonic scale

D-pentatonic scale

E-pentatonic scale

So now we have doubled up the number of notes to use when improvising. It might seem a bit overwhelming with all those new tones. But as you'll see after going through the next examples, it won't be a problem. Just add the new notes one by one.

I've written out six examples in which I demonstrate the use of the new material. Step by step I'll extend the well-known "one octave scales" and step by step the exercises will turn into music. Keep in mind that playing these examples is an excellent way to learn these new areas of the scales. The licks mainly start on the root tone of the scale but I've also added some licks starting on the major 3rd and the perfect 5th. The most important thing right now is not to move too fast. Take your time and try to use the process of picturing the scales too.

22

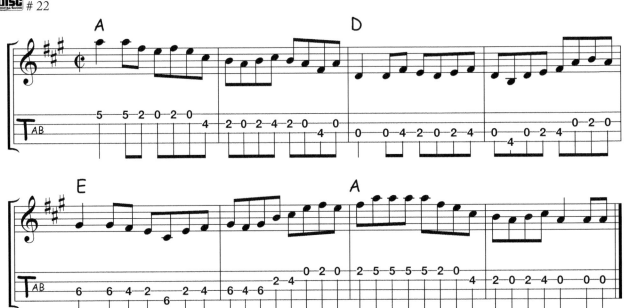

 # 23

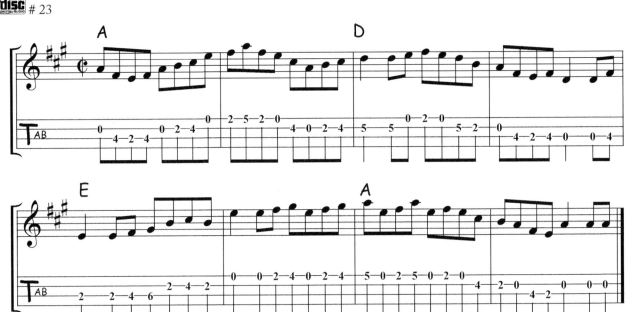

 # 24

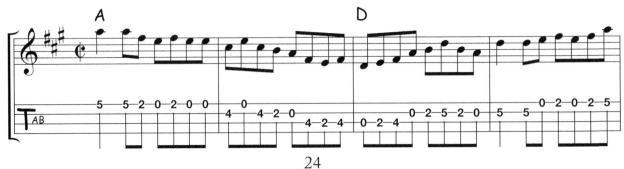

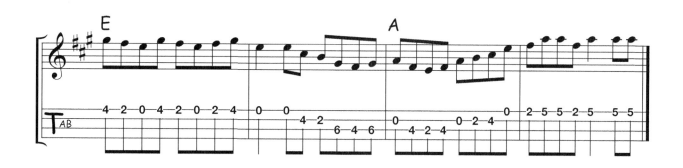

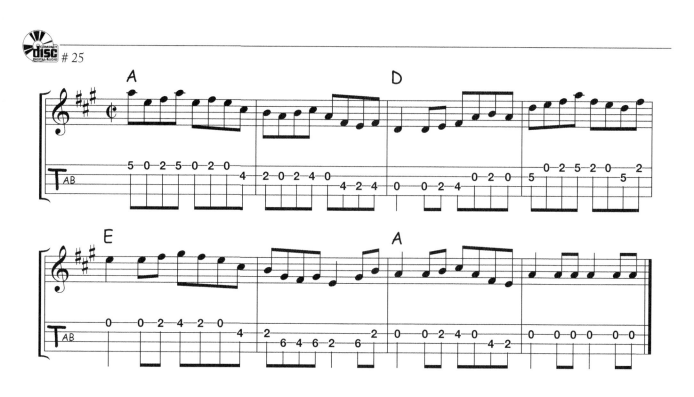

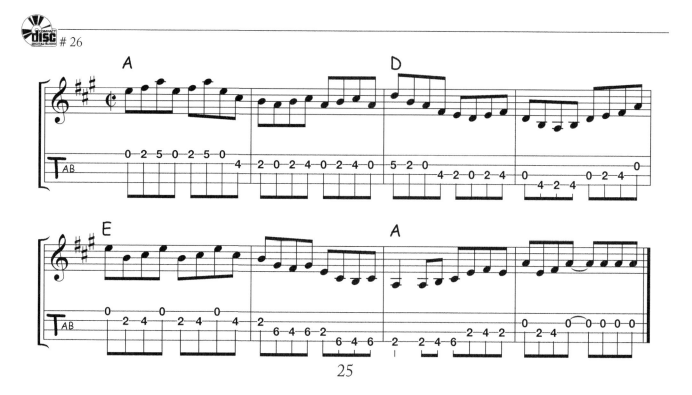

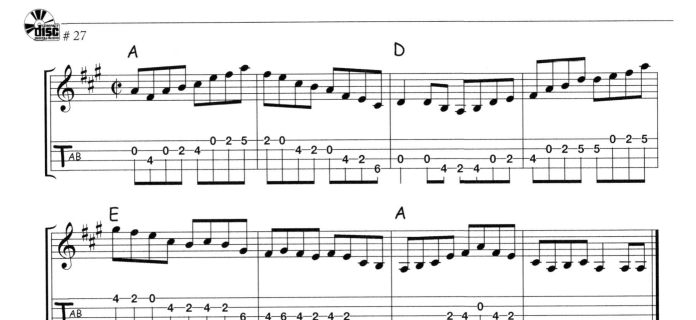

ASSIGNMENTS

1. Write out a nice sounding A-pentatonic lick.
2. Write out a hot burning D-pentatonic lick.
3. Write out a good playable E-pentatonic lick.

CHAPTER 6: Slow Improvising

Until now we have focused on learning and picturing the pentatonic scales. The next step will be to take the things we have already learned and apply them to the technique called slow improvising. As you might have guessed, it's time to slow down the process of improvising. In fact, we have to get so slow that we even don't need our mandolin at first. Take a piece of standard notation/tablature paper and a pen. And once again it's time to find a quiet undisturbed place for "studying."

Instead of slow improvising, we could also name this technique "the system of composing a solo, the way that it sounds like an improvised solo." A long title, but quite informative.

Before we start composing, I have a couple of small rules you need to keep in mind. For the first, you need to pick out some licks that you would like to use for the slow improvising. Two for each chord might be enough. Use material from the previous chapters mixed up with some of your own composed licks. The most difficult thing about slow improvising is the connection or transition between the licks, which needs to be as smooth as possible. The next example will show you what you **shouldn't do.**

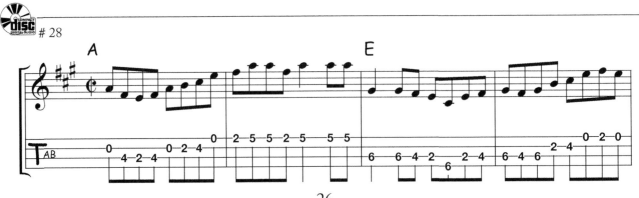

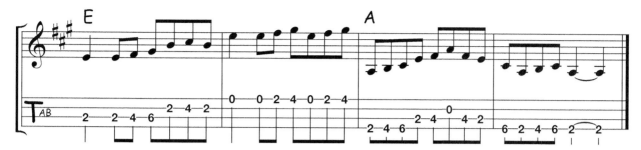

As you could hear, it didn't sound particular good, jumping around between the licks. The next choice will illustrate the right way to do it.

29

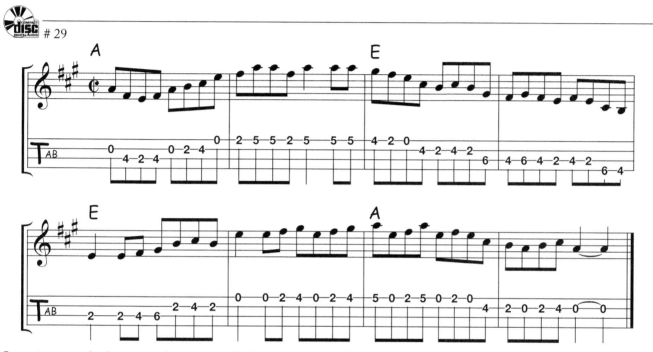

Sometimes we also have to make some small changes to some of the last notes in the lick to make it fit the beginning of the next lick better. In the following two examples, I'll show you how a "non-smooth lick-connection" could be managed by changing only a couple of notes.

30

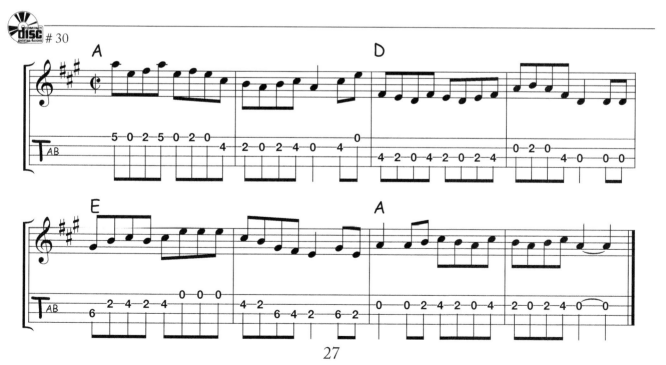

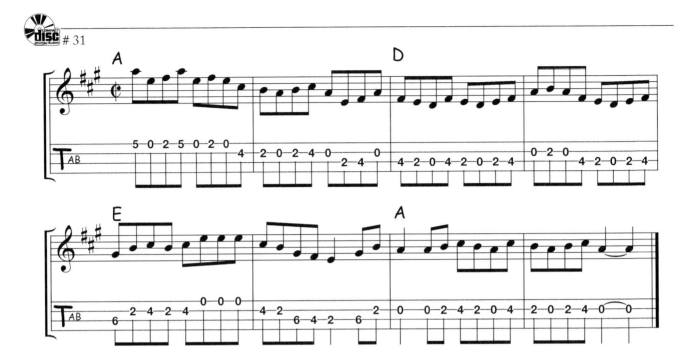

For the assignments we'll use the following chord progression.

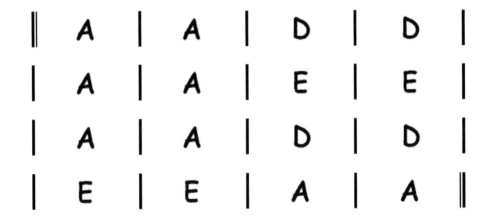

ASSIGNMENTS

1. Use the system of slow improvising on the chord progression above. Use as many of your favorite pentatonic licks as possible. It is all right to use a lick more than once in your composed solo. You might have to recompose the ending of some of the licks, to make them fit together better.

2. Repeat the process with the same chord progression, using some of the same licks as before, but change the order in which they are played.

3. Try the system on another chord progression.

Slow improvisation is like doing a puzzle. Sometimes, the licks just fit each other perfectly and other times it's really not that easy. But trust me! This system will help you on your way. It makes you memorize your licks better, because you have to use them when composing your solo. That's a big step in the right direction.

In slow improvisation, we learned about the importance of making a smooth connection between the licks. We have also started to collect some favorite licks, from our "bag of licks."

All improvisers have a "bag of licks," containing a handful of licks they like to use when improvising. Some of the licks might be "fancy-hot-burning" and some others might be more neutral sounding. The last category of licks is the most important when beginning to improvise. The reason for this is quite simple. A more neutral sounding lick can be played more often than the hot one. A hot lick is more recognizable if you play it over and over again while improvising. The neutral one isn't. Boring facts, but it's the truth.

O.K. let's not worry about the boring facts above. Let's jump to a new technique called stationary improvisation. Stationary improvisation takes its basis in only one chord, in contrast to slow improvisation, where improvisation is used over more chords.

Good improvisers are all able to draw ideas from their "bag of licks" while playing music. This procedure doesn't give them much time to consider the next draw. But well-trained improvisers don't need that much time and the drawing process becomes more or less automatic. To learn this, we have to start training our speed in drawing licks. While going through the next assignments, the system of stationary improvisation will become clearer to you.

ASSIGNMENTS

In the following assignments, we'll put all our attention on playing over the A chord. To make these exercises work, it's very important only to make use of memorized licks, instead of reading from the tablature.

1. Pick out two of your favorite A-pentatonic licks. Try to combine your licks with arpeggio-based playing (see Chapter 2) using the following system: Two bars of lick 1 – two bars of A arpeggio – two bars of lick 2 – and then two bars of A arpeggio – etc. Try to keep the arpeggios easily playable and use them as a bridge between your licks.

2. Add another lick to your playing, using the system: Lick 1 – arpeggio - lick 2 – arpeggio - lick 3 – arpeggio – etc.

3. Change the order of the licks.

4. Try the system on licks for the D and the E chord.

5. Instead of using arpeggios, try out the system using "easy playing" (see the upcoming chapter).

The following assignments should only be played by mandolin players who know their licks by heart. If you're still uncertain playing your licks, the following exercises might make everything worse. Spend more time practicing your licks to perfection. After this, you'll be able to manage the following exercises.

6. Play one of your favorite licks twice. The second time, force yourself to do a small variation. Play this exercise in a circle. Lick – variation – lick - variation – etc.

7. Repeat the exercise with another lick of yours.

8. Try to play stationary using different licks or lick variations only. If you get lost, play some arpeggio style or "easy playing" in order to make the exercise move.

The more licks you have in your "bag of licks," the easier it will be to play over a stationary chord. Try to make a habit out of this exercise, it's well worth the effort, believe me!

When you reach the point where the "drawing" of licks starts to become easier, it's time to start improvising in real time (but at a slow tempo). To prepare you for improvising in real time, I've made a list containing some of the main problems my students have had over the years. I've also tried to figure out some answers to the problems.

Problem 1:   To be able to remember the chord progression while improvising.

Solution: To solve this problem, it's very important not to work on chord progressions that are too difficult in the beginning. Use only chord progressions in which the chords change every two measures. It's always a good idea to write down the chord changes on a sheet of paper. Then try to memorize the tune in four-bar segments, for example: I A I A I D I D I - then - I E I E I A I A I - etc. This system of "memorizing in segments" will train one to be able to look forward in the tune while improvising.

Problem 2:   To be able to draw licks, one after each other, - continuous and flowing.

Solution: Our improvisation doesn't have to contain licks only. Everybody who's learning to improvise gets "blackouts" sometimes. We know what chord is coming up, but we just can't remember a lick to play at that very moment. In a spot like this, it's quite important to continue the soloing. But what should we play?! I'll tell you. Play something easy. Play a "double-stop shuffle" (see Chapter 3) or stay for a while on a chord-tone. You could also play a short, improvised pentatonic melody– try something out (it might work). It's better to play "something" than to leave a space in the solo. Lots of improvisers do not play licks only. They combine licks with "easy playing." To demonstrate this, I've written out an example in which I change between two bars of licks and two bars of "easy playing." As you can see, "easy playing" basically means playing fewer notes with less ornamentation.

32

30

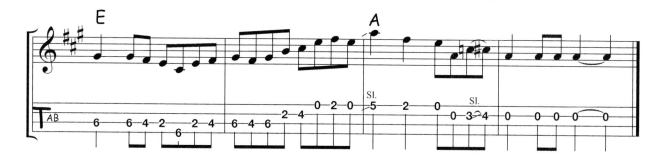

Problem 3:   To consider on which note we should start the following lick (while playing).

Solution: In Chapter 6 (slow improvising), we learned about the importance of a smooth connection between the licks. To do this while improvising in real time isn't that easy. The most important rule is not to jump too much around. Try to find a lick that starts close to the last note in the lick you have just played. The more licks you know and the more you know how to vary them, the easier it will be to connect the licks. The connection lines in Chapter 9 will also help us to master this problem.

Problem 4:   What to do when you "get lost."

Solution: To "get lost" while improvising isn't much fun. You don't know where you are in the chord progression and on which chord you should play. Now you have two possibilities. You can stop playing and let another musician take over, or you can try to get back on the track. If you choose the last choice, you have to play "something" as in problem 2. Don't try to play licks if you "got lost." Use the pentatonic scale of the key played (Ex: A-major → A-pentatonic). Play around this scale using two or three notes. Stay on a note if it sounds good. While "playing around," try to figure out where in the chord progression you are. Over the years I've seen people "get lost" while improvising. Some of them stopped playing and others continued. It was not always a pleasure listening to those who continued, but I've always admired their courage. Don't be afraid of trying something out. And don't forget– those who had the courage to continue, even though they "got lost," were also those who, later on, became good improvisers. In the assignments of this chapter I'll give you an exercise in which you can practice "playing around" while "being lost."

Problem 5:   Even though you know a lot of licks, you feel like you are repeating the same licks all the time.

Solution: This isn't a big problem. It's more a phase you have to get past. Play some more exercises, using your other licks. Time will solve this problem.

Problem 6:   After improvising over a chord progression for a while, you're not improvising any more. You have composed a solo (while playing), instead of improvising by using different licks.

Solution: By composing a solo (while playing), you just took "slow improvising" a step further. If you needed a composed solo for that chord progression, you did a good job. But if you're training in improvising, you should change to a new chord progression, before "composing."

Problem 7:   To be able to improvise over six or eight bars of the same chord.

Solution: If you have been practicing stationary improvising, you already know how to play over more bars of the same chord. Instead of counting the bars, try to think in lick segments. Four bars = two licks, Six bars = three licks, etc. If you don't feel comfortable with stationary improvising yet, you could also use the lick combined with the "easy playing" system: Play a two bar lick, then two bars of "easy playing," and then a lick (two bars), etc.

31

ASSIGNMENTS

1. As a warm-up exercise, try to improvise over an easy chord progression. Force your self to use "easy playing." Try to improvise small pentatonic melodies using the pentatonic scale belonging to the chord played. Add some "double-stop shuffles" if you like. But don't use any licks at all! This exercise will help you if you need to play "something" while improvising or by collecting ideas for "easy playing." After the assignment I'll show you an example in which only "easy playing" is used.

2. This exercise is the "I got lost" exercise. Choose an easy chord progression (in the key a A-major) from the CD. Try to improvise over the changes using only the A-pentatonic scale. Normally we'll change pentatonic scale on the D and the E chord, but in this exercise we don't. If you "get lost," you don't know what chord is played and what pentatonic-scale to use. In the key of A-major, the A-pentatonic scale is the scale having the most common tones. The notes e and b of the A-pentatonic scale will fit the E chord and the notes f♯ and a will fit the D chord. This exercise might not sound bluegrassy at all, but it will help you to "survive" if you "get lost."

3. Apply the "I got lost tools" on another chord progression. Choose a measure in the middle of the progression in which you'd like to start using your licks. Play around the A-pentatonic scale (surviving) until you arrive at the chosen measure. Then start playing your licks. After playing for a while, choose a different measure to "get back on the track."

4. Improvise over an easy chord progression (in a slow tempo). Use the lick combined with an "easy playing" system as already learned. Two bars of lick – two bars of "easy playing" – two bars of lick – etc.

5. Try to improvise using licks only. Focus on getting a smooth connection between the licks. Try not to "get lost" – but, if you do, you know what to do.

It's a good idea to practice improvising together with another musician who's on the same level as yourself. Change back and forth, between being the accompanist and being the improviser. Don't play too fast!

I promised to show you an example, in which only "easy playing" is used. I tried to mix up pentatonic scales with chord-tones and other small ideas. Check out how the use of slides can make "easy playing" sound more interesting. Some of the last ideas in this example might not be so "easy" to play because of the slide to the 7th fret. I chose to add those ideas to the example, because of the fact that they sound good as "fill in licks" between other kinds of licks. The slide to the root of the chord (7th fret) gives us a kind of old-time fiddle sound, which is often used on the chords A, D and E.

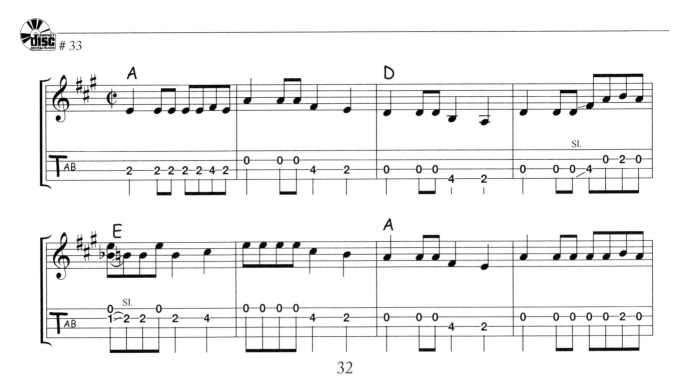

32

33

CHAPTER 9: The Spices

Now it's time to go a step further in our improvisation study. It's time to add the spices to the soup. In the previous chapters, we have been working on learning the pentatonic scales. We have done some exercises which helped us become familiar with those five-note scales and we have started to collect ideas for our "bag of licks." In this chapter we'll start to extend our pentatonic scales with some new note material. "The spices" will make our licks sound more interesting and in some cases, even make some of the lines technically easier to play.

In all of the following examples, we'll start focusing a bit more on the theory. When you learn a lick, it's a good idea to know what's going on. Why does the lick sound the way it does? If you understand the theory behind the licks, it will help you in many ways. You'll find it easier to transpose licks into other keys. You'll be able to analyze licks from your favorite mandolin players. And you'll also be able to compose licks yourself, using the ideas you like.

The minor 3rd (♭3)

The first note to add will be the minor 3rd, which we already know from the minor arpeggios in Chapter 2. In the following examples, we won't use the ♭3 in order to give us a minor sound, but as a leading note, leading to the note a half step above or below. This way of using the ♭3 is very common in bluegrass. In the tablature, I've marked the spots where the minor 3rd is used, with the sign: ♭3.

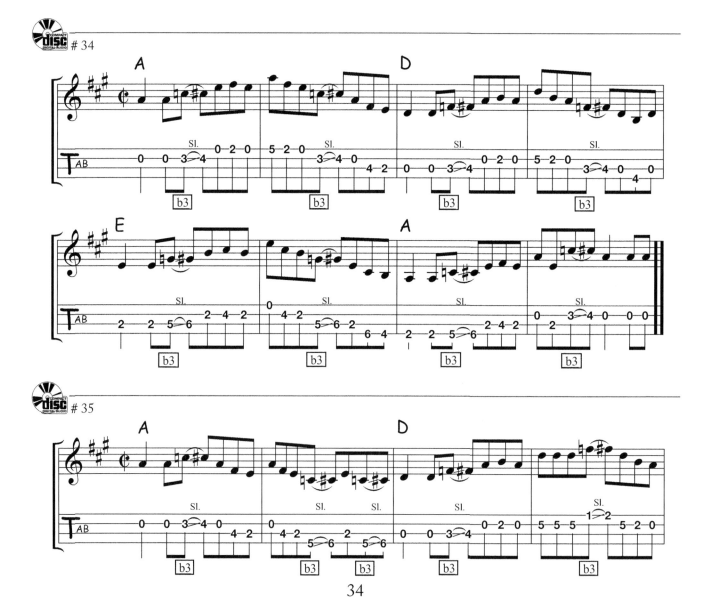

34

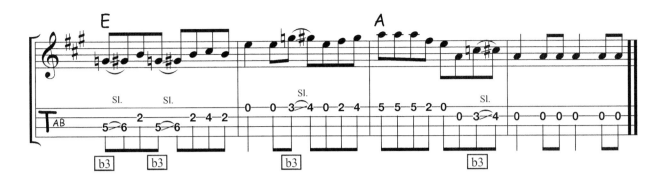

36

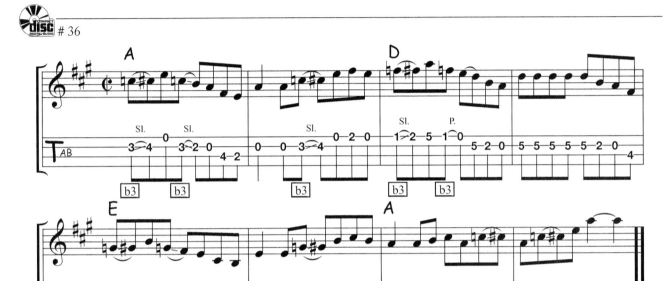

37

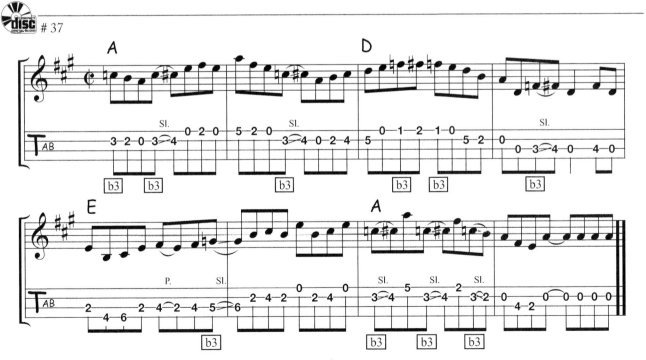

35

The minor 7th (♭7)

Another common sound in bluegrass is the flatted seventh sound (♭7). It gives us a bluesy sound, which could be used in different kinds of bluegrass tunes. As you probably already guessed, the minor 7th will be marked like this: ♭7

 # 38

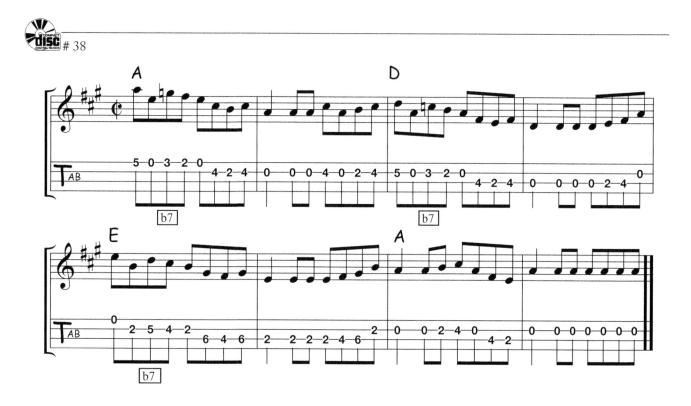

 # 39

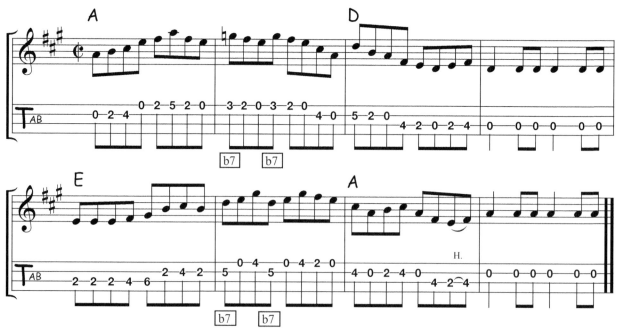

36

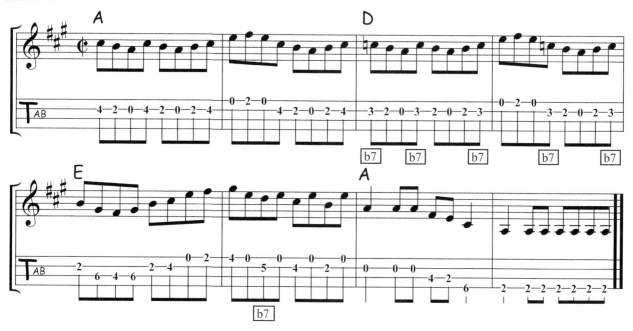

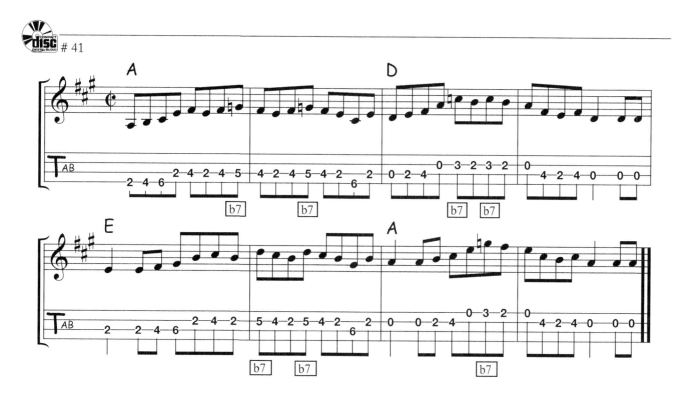

The perfect 4th (P4)

The perfect 4th is nearly always used in connection with the major 3rd or the perfect 5th. It's not a note you should stay on for a long time. Use it as a passing tone and it will work perfectly. By adding the P4 to the E-pentatonic scale, we give ourself a new open string to play. It makes improvisation over the E chord much more comfortable. The E-pentatonic scale and the perfect 4th are kind of "made for each other" and commonly used by improvisers. Every time we have the possibility to use an open string, it's a relief.

37

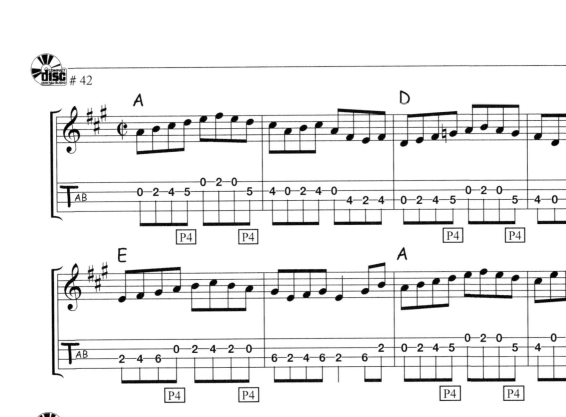

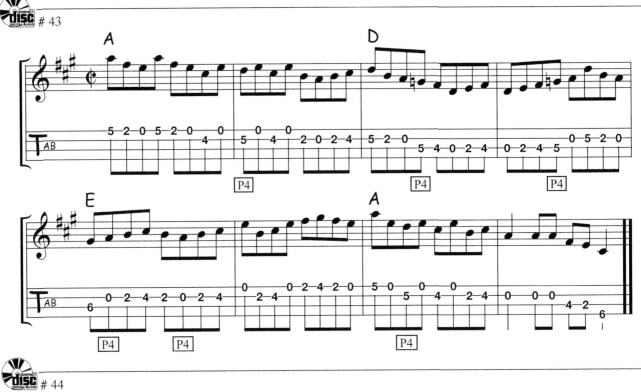

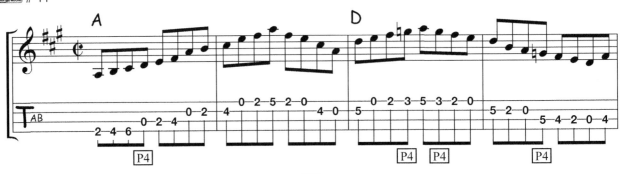

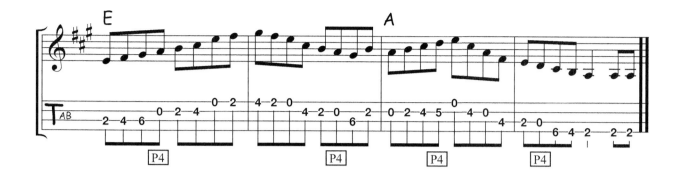

The major 7th (M7)

In the next examples the major 7th is used as a leading tone, leading to the root. Standing alone, the major 7th would give the music a jazzy touch, which in this case, isn't commonly used in bluegrass.

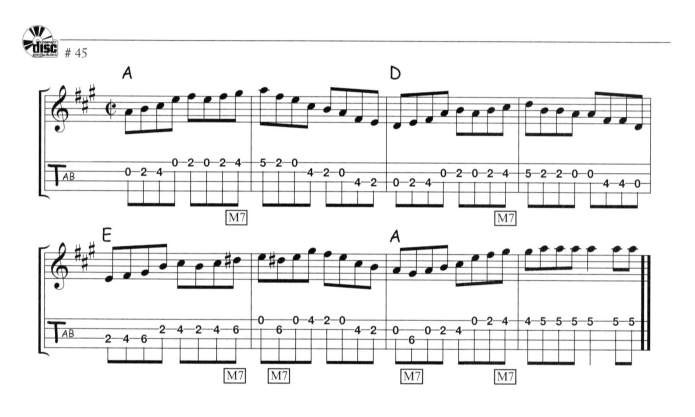

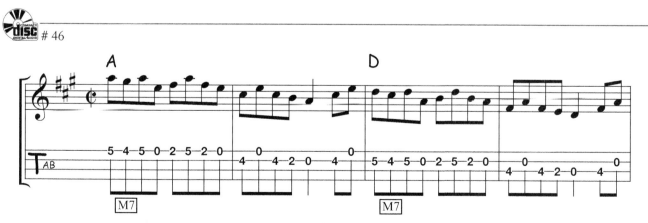

39

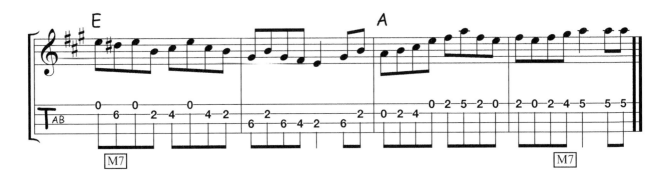

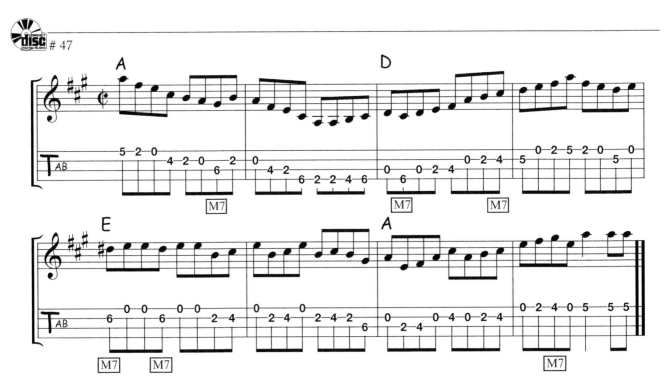

Connection lines (C-L)

Another common improvisation tool is the use of connection lines. The idea is to play something that makes the transition between two chords smooth and interesting at the same time. At the end of a lick, we'll play one or more tones, which leads us into the next chord. These notes would almost always belong to the tonality of the following chord. This might give us some disharmony, but because of the leading effect, it won't sound wrong.

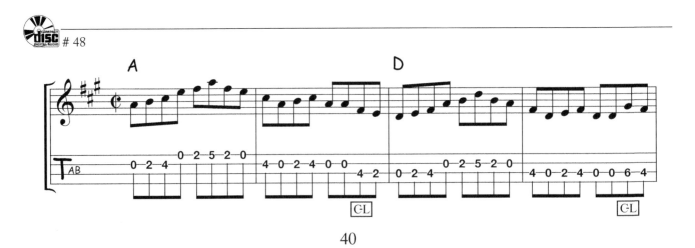

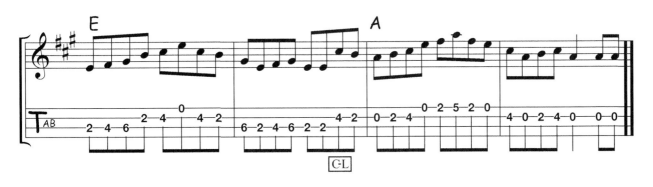

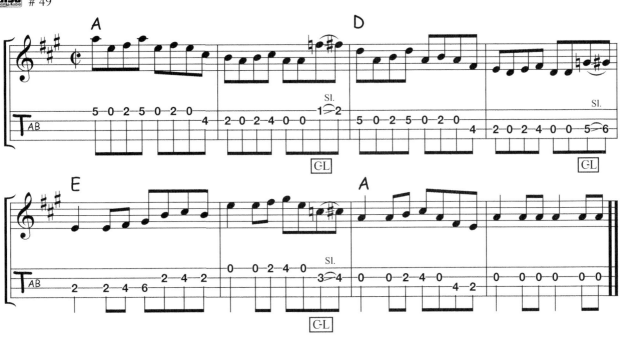

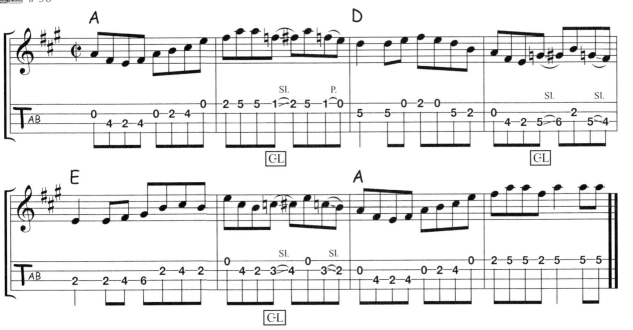

41

While playing the examples in this chapter, you'll also learn the sound of the new improvisation material. It will make you grow as a musician and you'll be able to recognize such things as a minor 7th or a minor 3rd leading to the major 3rd when they are played. It will also help you transcribe licks or solos from recordings.

ASSIGNMENTS

1. Compose some new licks, using the "spices."

2. Analyze the following lick:

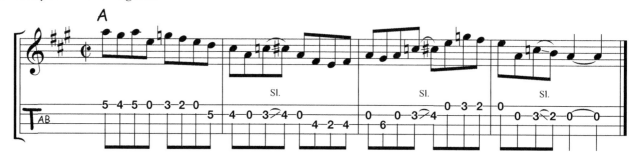

CHAPTER 10: Mixing the Ideas

In this chapter I've written out some solos mixing up the material we've learned in the previous chapters. It's important not only to play the solos, but also to analyze them afterwards.

51

Solo 1

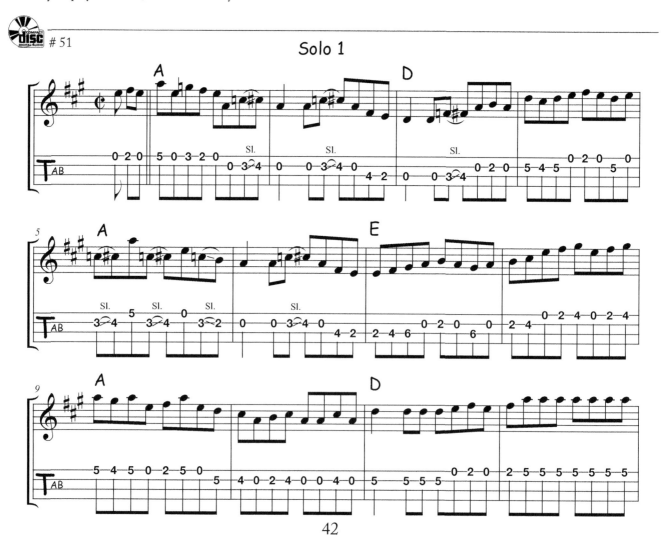

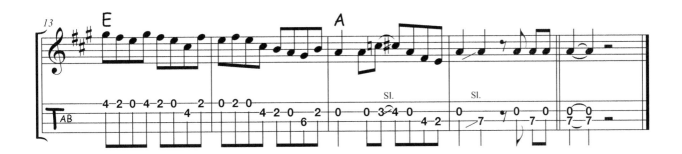

Solo 2

43

Solo 3

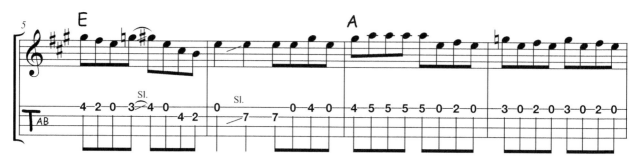

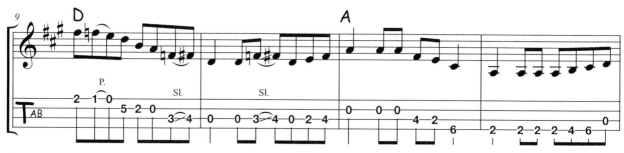

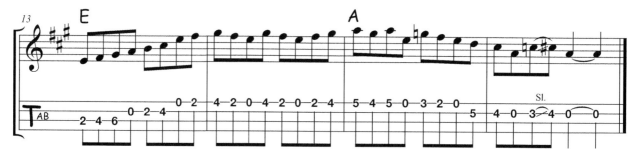

Solo 4

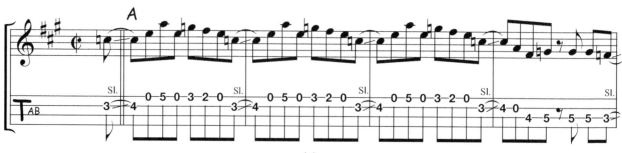

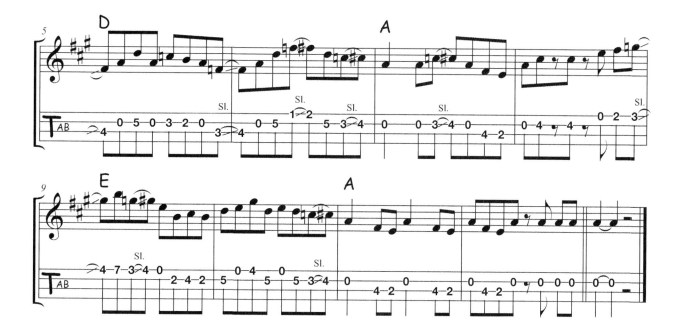

ASSIGNMENTS

1. Pick out some licks for your "bag of licks."

2. Use the system of slow improvisation on some other chord progressions. Make use of licks from the four written out solos mixed with material already played.

CHAPTER 11: One-bar Licks

In order to keep the learning process more clear, we've only been working with two-bar licks until now. But as improvisers, we should also be able to handle one-bar licks.

Let's take a look at one of the two-bar licks we have already played. Maybe we could split the lick into two one-bar licks.

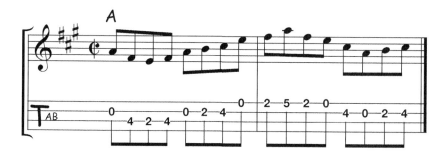

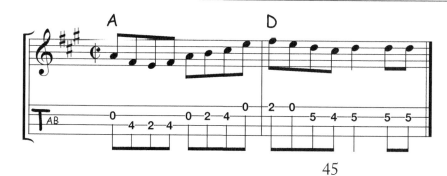

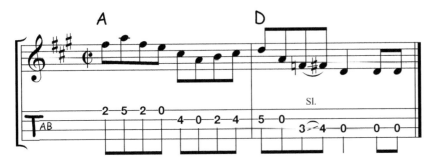

Nearly all two-bar licks can be split into two one-bar licks. In the following example, I've composed a short solo using ideas from the material already played.

55

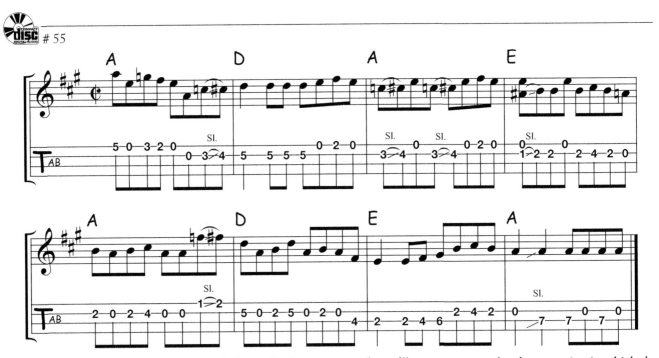

To improvise over one-bar changes is a challenge. In the next example you'll see a common chord progression in which the use of one-bar licks is necessary.

56

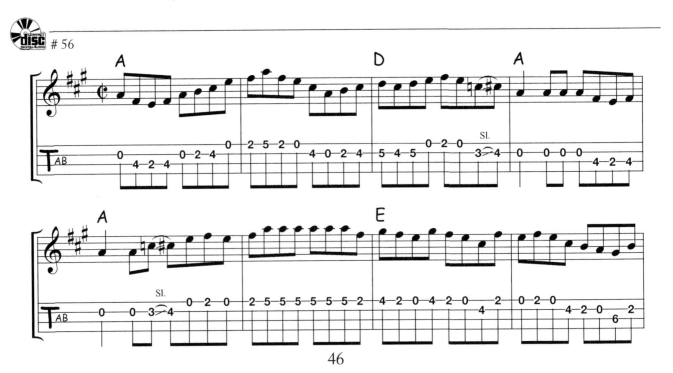

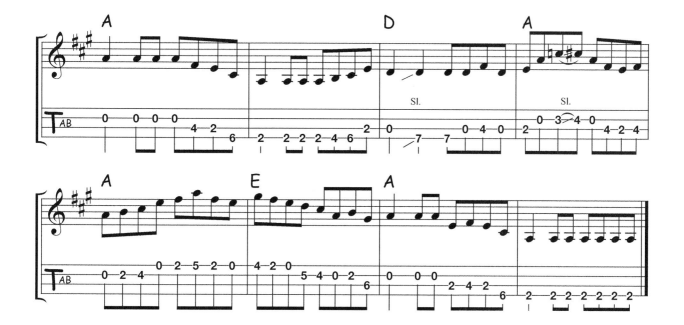

ASSIGNMENTS

1. Compose a couple of licks fitting the following one-bar changes: | D | A | and | A | E |

2. Try to improvise on the chord progression used in the last example (See the appendix to find the jam-track on the CD). On the one-bar changes, make use of the licks you just composed.

CHAPTER 12: "Last Line" Licks

A very common "last line" in lots of bluegrass songs goes like this:

| A | E | A | A |

This ending is so common that improvisers often have some licks fitting this progression. The following example will show you a couple of composed "last line" licks using ideas from the previous chapters.

57

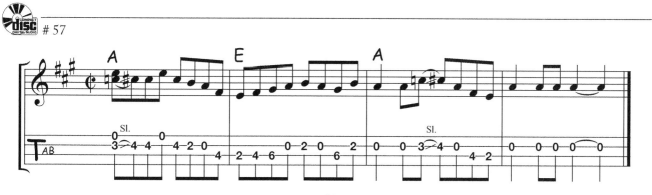

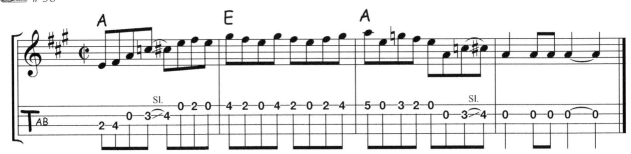

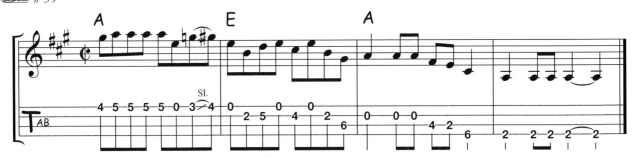

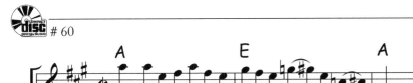

A very important spot in these "last line" licks, is the third bar. I call this bar our "home." While improvising, we make a lot of movements, the fingers are walking around on the fingerboard exploring different areas. But after our "adventure" we need to come home. At the very end of the chord progression (on the third bar of the last line) it sounds good if we're "landing" on the root of the key. We're coming "home" (home sweet home). I also "landed" on the root in the examples just played. It's quite common to "land" on the first beat of the bar, but a small delay could also be used as shown in the next examples.

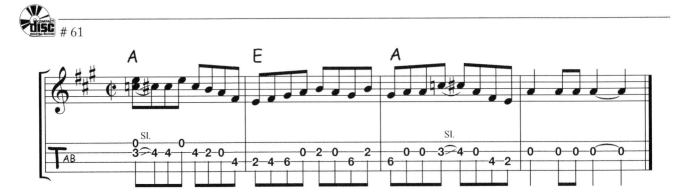

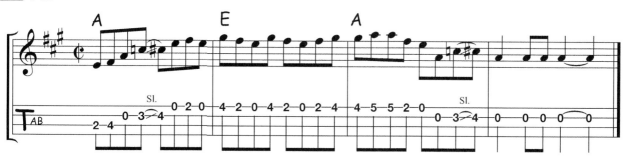

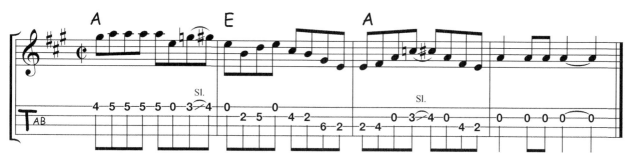

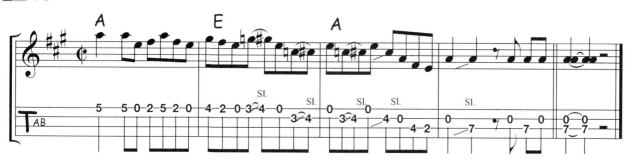

Another trick to use on "last line" licks, is the "let's forget about the E chord" trick. In fact we'll just act as if we are improvising over four bars of A-major. We can permit ourselves to forget about the E chord. But, - and this is very important: We need to come "home" on the third bar. Check out the following examples!

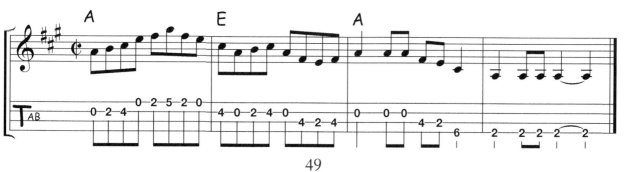

49

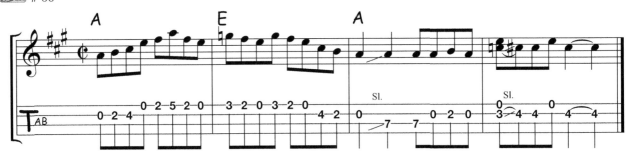

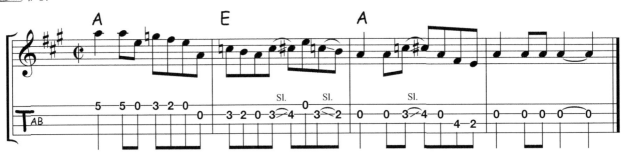

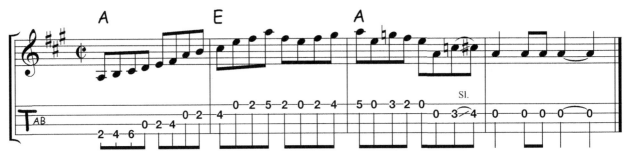

ASSIGNMENTS

1. Learn some of the "last line" licks by heart.

2. Try to compose some "last line" licks yourself.

CHAPTER 13: The G Chord

Now at this point, it's time to take a look at some other chords and the associated arpeggios, scales and "spices." The first chord we'll work on is the G chord. As in the previous chapters, we need to learn our new improvising material step by step. We'll do the process of picturing the shape of the pentatonic scale and we'll also add some "spices to the soup." Because of the limited sound of the one-octave scales, we'll only work with the scales in their two-octave forms from now on.

But first, let's play the G-major arpeggio in order to know where the chord tones are. As in Chapter 2, we'll play the arpeggio like this: Root → major 3rd → perfect 5th.

50

G-major arpeggio

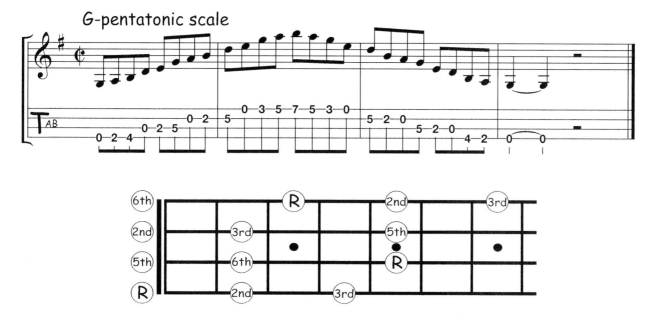

The G-pentatonic scale is quite easy to play because of the use of the four open strings. While playing the next example, try to memorize the shape of the scale. Look at the box system and use this as help to picture the scale.

G-pentatonic scale

In order to become familiar with this scale, I've written out eight bars of stationary pentatonic playing. Play the example and enjoy its playability.

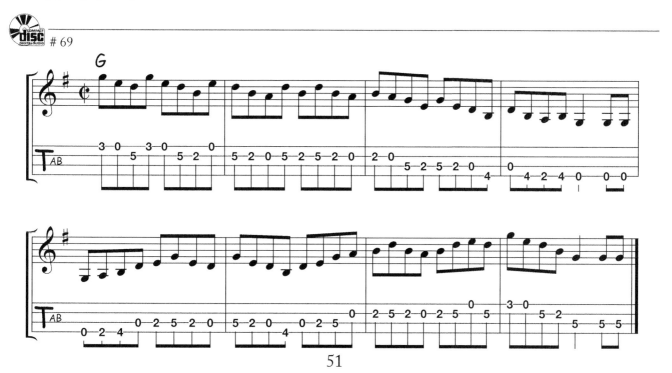

69

G

51

Notice that every D-lick that we have been playing on the three highest strings can be transposed to the G chord by playing the lick one string lower, as is done in the next examples:

In the following examples we'll add some "spices" to the G-pentatonic scale.

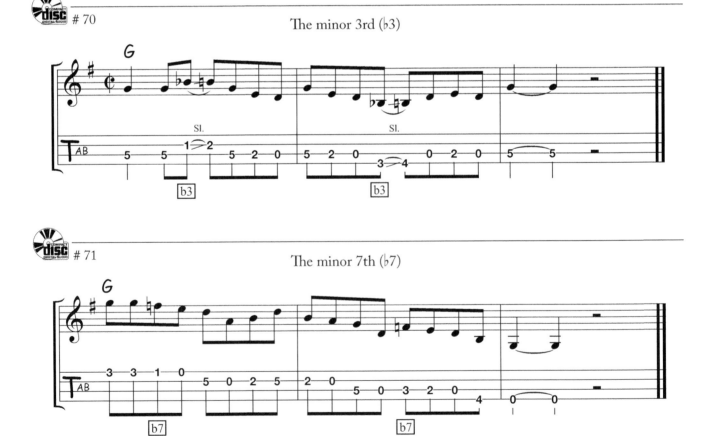

The perfect 4th (P4)

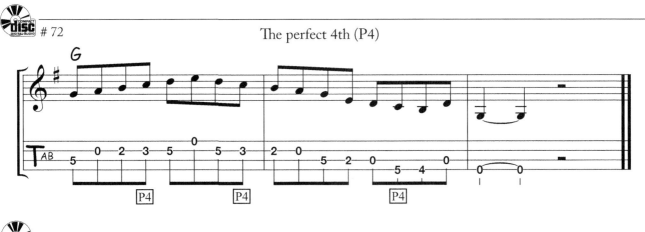

The major 7th (M7)

To demonstrate the connection lines, I've used the chord connection D to G.

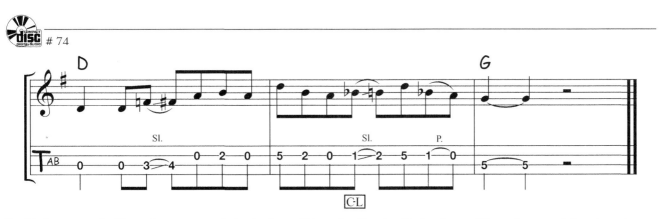

In this last example, I've written out a solo in the key of D-major. For the G chord, we will use the material we have just learned.

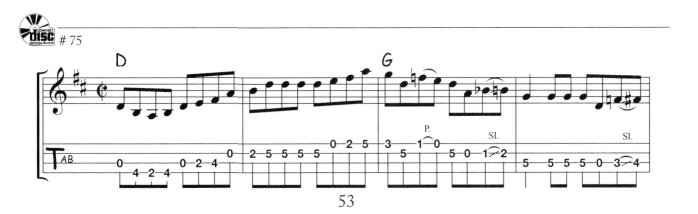

ASSIGNMENTS

1. Compose a couple of G licks.

2. Improvise or compose a solo over the following chord progression in the key of G-major.

E	E	A	A
D	D	G	G

3. Improvise or compose a solo over the following chord progression in the key of D-major. Even though we have a D7 chord in the third line, it's not necessary to play that chord differently. If you want to emphasize the D7 sound, then you can add the ♭7 "spice" to the D-pentatonic scale at that spot.

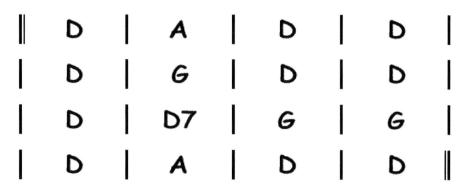

D	A	D	D
D	G	D	D
D	D7	G	G
D	A	D	D

4. Write out one more "last line" lick in the key of D-major.

| | D | A | D | D ||

5. Write out one more "last line" lick in the key of G-major.

| | G | D | G | G ||

CHAPTER 14: The C Chord

With the G chord tools that we have just learned, we made it possible to improvise in the key of D-major. But if we want to play something in the key of G-major, we need to learn some tools to use for improvising over the C chord. After G and D, the C chord would be the most common chord used when playing a song in the key of G-major.

O.K. as a warm up exercise, let's play the C-major arpeggio the same as we did in the last chapter with the G chord– you know: Root → major 3rd → perfect 5th .

C-major arpeggio

Also the C-pentatonic scale is quite easy to play, because of the fact that four open strings belong to the scale. So once again it is time for playing, memorizing and visualizing.

C-pentatonic scale

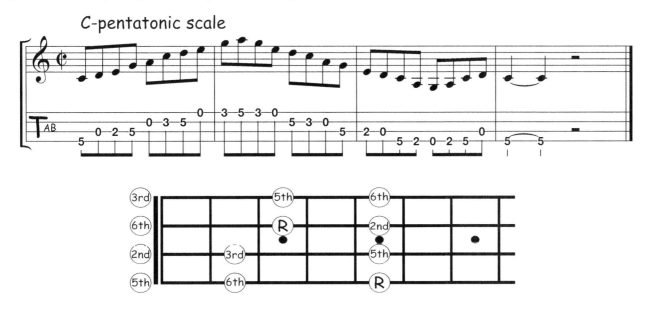

For the C chord, I've also written out eight bars of stationary pentatonic playing for you to work on. As you can see, I've added a high c-tone to the scale (first note/second line). This means that we have to change position in order to be able to reach that spot.

55

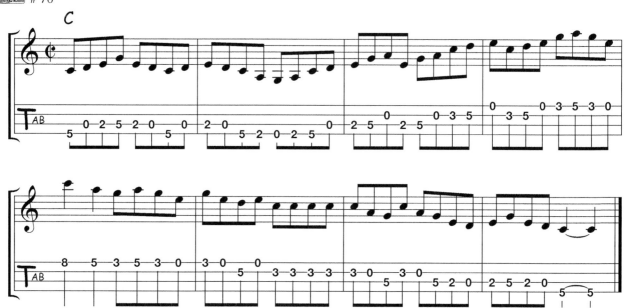

The following solo in the key of G-major uses only pentatonic scales. Feel free to do some variations with the D chord if the pure pentatonic scale sounds too boring to you.

 # 77

Solo 1

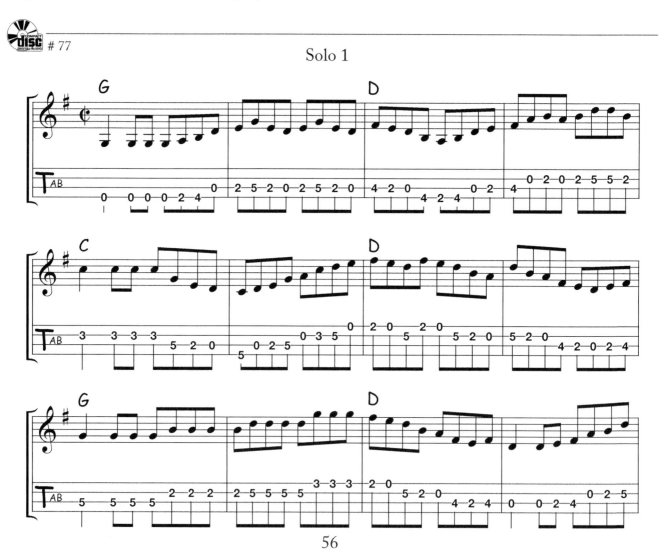

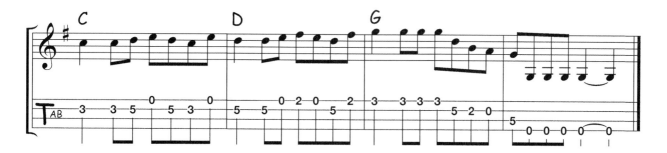

The most common chords in the key of C-major are C, F and G. To avoid the F chord, which we haven't covered yet, I've written out a solo in C-major, in which only the C and the G chords are used. In order to learn the "spices" belonging to the C chord, I've added as many as possible to this solo. As you can see, the solo also contains some "easy playing."

78

Solo 2

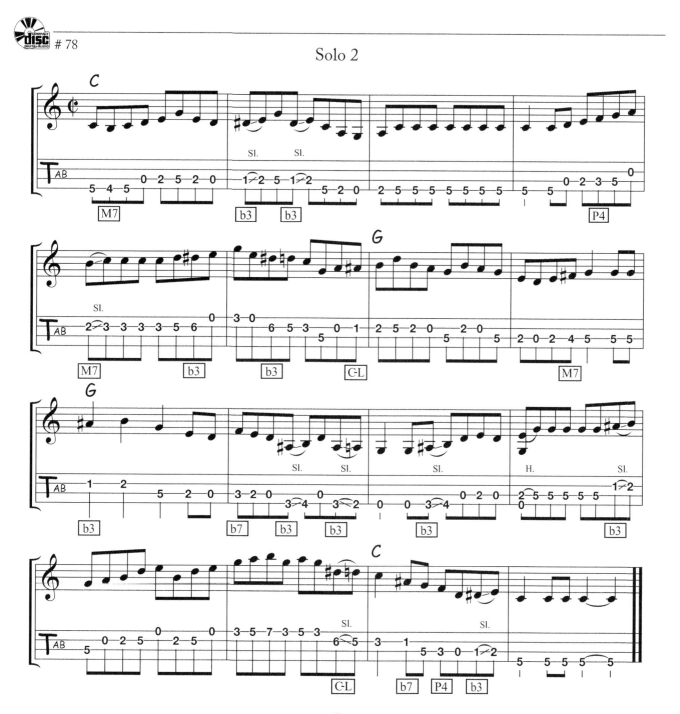

57

ASSIGNMENTS

1. Compose a couple of C licks.

2. Improvise or compose a solo over the following chord progression in the key of G-major.

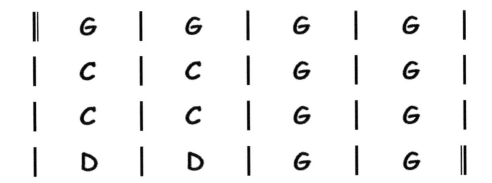

3. Write out one more "last line" lick in the key of C-major.

CHAPTER 15: The F Chord

The last chord in the key of C-major for which we need some tools is the F chord and as you already might have guessed, we'll start out by playing the F chord arpeggio.

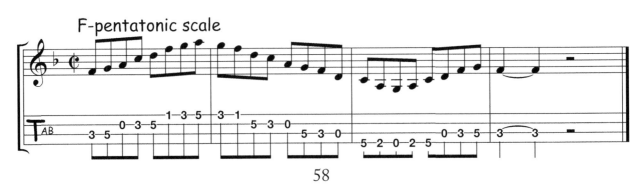

F-major arpeggio

And now let's play the pentatonic scale.

F-pentatonic scale

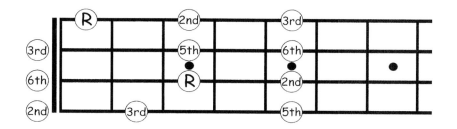

In order to illustrate the F-pentatonic scale in use, I've written out a small solo in the key of C-major. To keep the solo more interesting, I allowed myself to add some "spices" to the C and the G chord (try to analyze those measures).

79

Solo 1

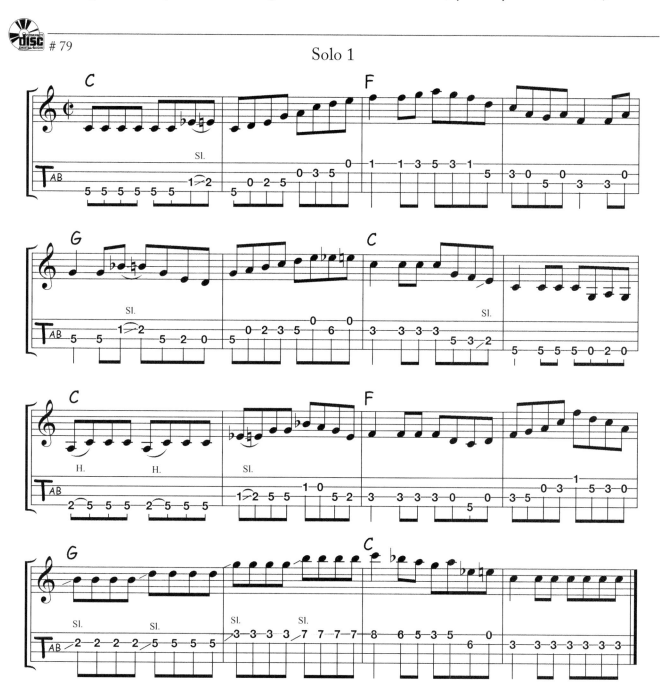

The pure F-pentatonic scale doesn't include the open E string, which makes this scale a little more difficult to play. But, don't worry! – it's actually no problem to add this tone to the pentatonic scale. The open E string would be the major 7th, a "spice" we already know from the previous chapters. As an example of this sound, check out the following lick:

59

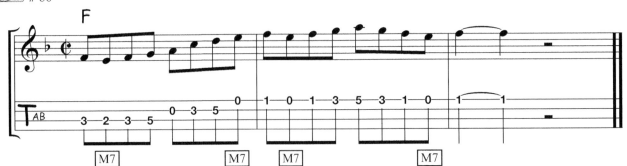

Until now, the major 7th was always played as a tone leading to the root of the chord. But in some cases, we could also play the major 7th as a passing tone between the root and the major 6th of the scale. This system won't sound correct for all chords, as I'll explain later on in Chapter 26 (Other Spices). But in the key of C-major, it sounds great to do this for the F chord as you will hear in this next example.

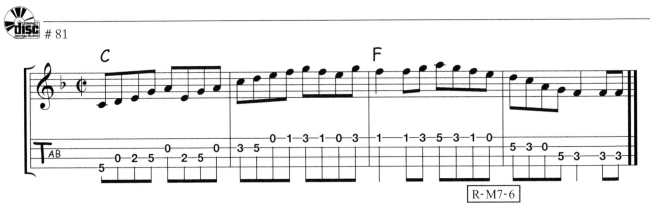

The last solo in this chapter will contain other "spices," to use with the F chord. As you can see, the use of the open E string on the F chord just makes playing more easy.

Solo 2

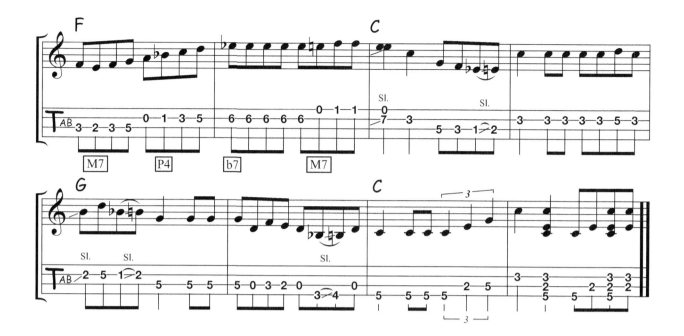

ASSIGNMENTS

1. Compose a couple of F licks.

2. Improvise or compose a solo over the following chord progression in the key of C-major.

CHAPTER 16: Other Major Chords

The scales that we have learned until now fit the six chords: A, D, E, G, C and F. These chords are all common chords in bluegrass music, but in order to be able to improvise in all common bluegrass keys, we also need some ideas for B♭-major and B-major.

B♭-major:

The three most commonly-used chords in B♭-major, are the B♭, E♭ and F chord. The fact that the b♭ note is placed a half-tone above the a-note makes construction of B♭ licks quite easy.
Every A chord lick that we have played until now could be transposed to B♭, simply by playing the tones one fret higher. This means that we have to change our finger position to be able to play the B♭ lick. Take a look at this A-pentatonic lick and how it can be transposed to B♭.

61

A-pentatonic lick

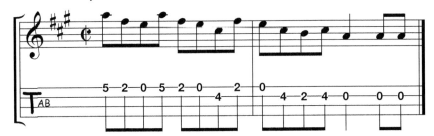

B♭-pentatonic lick

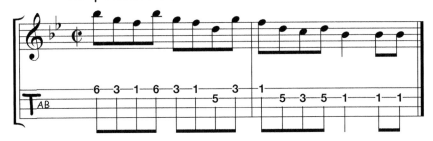

The chords D and E in A-major could also be transposed to E♭ and F, by using the same system of moving up one fret. The E-pentatonic scale contains the note: g♯ (d string/6th fret) which will be turned into the a note (d string/7th fret) when moving up to F. Obviously this note could also be played as an open string, as you can see in this example:

E-pentatonic lick

F-pentatonic lick 1

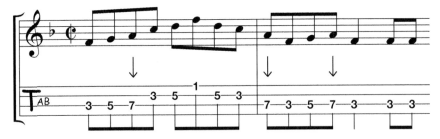

F-pentatonic lick 2

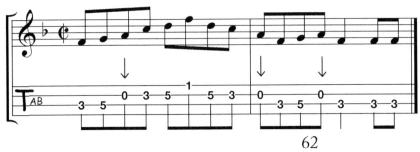

The next examples will show us how the material we have already played sounds when it's transposed to Bb-major. The first example came from Chapter 4 and only used one-octave pentatonic scales. The last example is taken from Chapter 5. With the Bb chord, it's also possible to make use of the open d string, which makes the lick easier to play.

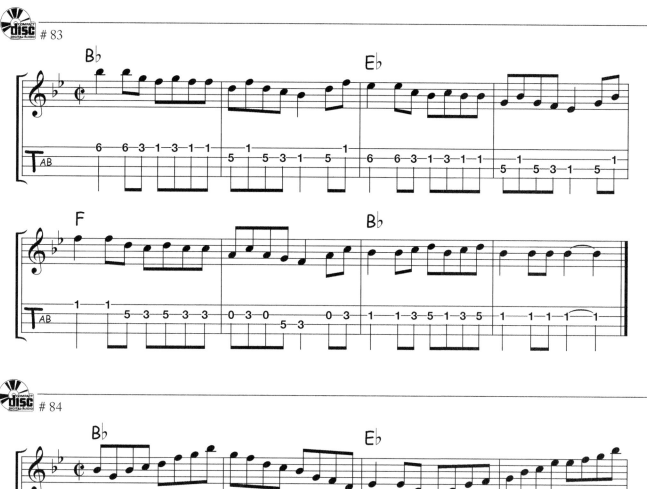

All in all, Bb-major might not be the easiest key to improvise over. Try to become familiar with the one-octave scales at first. Don't push your self too hard. If you find that some of the licks come out uncomfortable to play, then try to recompose them and make them playable.

B-major:

In the key of B-major, it's possible to use the same transposing system as we did for Bb-major. Instead of transposing every

A-major note up a half-tone (one fret), we need to use whole-tone steps (two frets). Check out how the examples we have already played from Chapters 4 and 5 sound in the key of B-major. The F♯-pentatonic scale is kind of tricky to play, but don't worry too much! Later I'll show you another way to play the F♯-pentatonic scale.

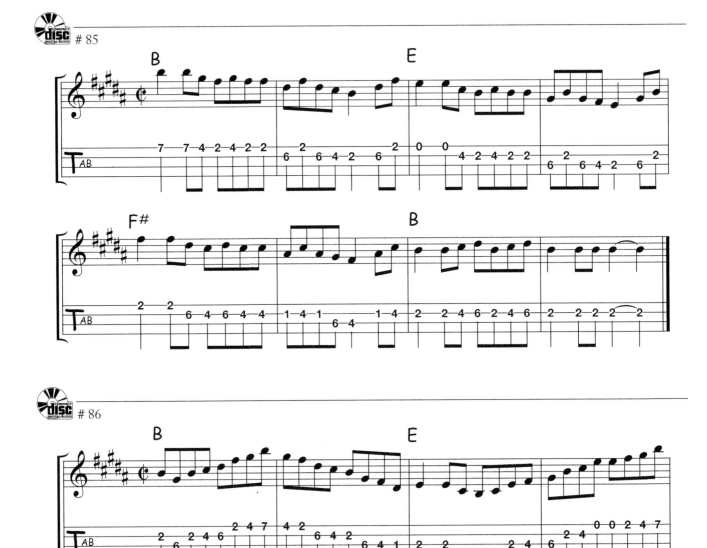

Transposing "up the neck":

Many improvisers utilize closed-position licks (no open strings). They jump from position to position, exploring the fingerboard and having fun. To reach this level, we need to know about these closed-position licks, and how to use them. The next example will illustrate how a D-pentatonic lick can be transposed "up the neck" to the chords: E♭, E, F, and F♯. Playing in closed position makes all licks similar to play. The difficult part is to learn to jump from one to another.

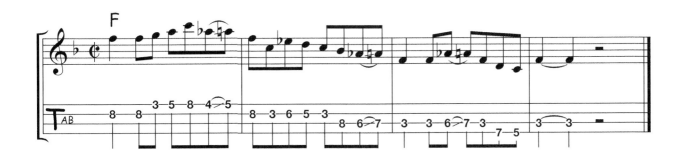

65

Check out this solo in the key of B-major. All licks are played in closed-position. I used a couple of spices in order to make the solo sound more interesting.

Solo

ASSIGNMENTS

1. Try to transpose some of your A chord licks up a half-tone (one fret).

2. Do the same with some of your D and E licks.

3. Some players prefer playing the F-pentatonic scale in closed position. What about you?

4. Try to transpose one of the solos in Chapter 10 into the key of B-major.

5. Figure out how the C-pentatonic scale could be played in closed position.

6. Compose a couple of good playable F♯ licks.

CHAPTER 17: Double-stops

In Chapter 3, we learned about the "double-stop shuffle" and how to use it as a substitute for a pentatonic lick. In this chapter I'll talk about the structure of the double-stops. We'll learn about improvising with the double-stops and how to move them up and down the neck.

As you probably remember, double-stops means two notes played together at the same time. Most of the time, these two notes are just plain chord tones belonging to the chord we need to improvise on. A very important thing when learning double-stops is the visualization of their structure. The chord for which we'll start learning the double-stops is the D chord. We have already played the D-major arpeggio in an earlier chapter, but to refresh our memories let's play it once again.

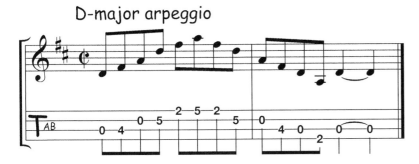

In the next example, I've written out the different double-stop possibilities we have when using the notes from the D-major arpeggio.

Structure 1:

In order to simplify the learning and the picturing of the double-stops, I would like to reduce the amount of shapes down to three. The following box system will show you the structure of the shapes. I call this structure: "Structure 1."

D chord positions

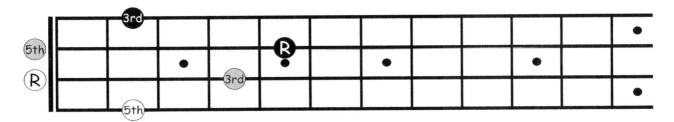

And now it's time to play our first double-stop lick. The idea is to move from one shape to another using all of the four strings going from high to low and back again.

67

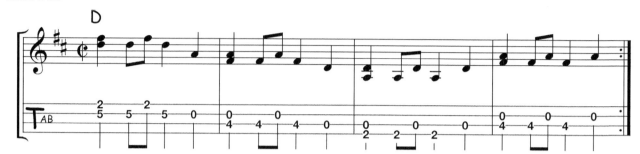

The next step is to move (transpose) the shapes up the neck, to the "E chord double-stop position." It means no open strings and a little stretch on the double-stop in the middle. If your fingers start to hurt while playing up the neck, then take a small break. Don't push your self too hard, but don't give up either– double-stops up the neck are learnable and very important to improvising. Check out the structure of the "E chord double-stop position" which is just a transposition of our D chord double-stop lick. Even though it might seem easier to start a lick with the second and the fourth finger, you should also try to use the first and the third instead. Why? – I'll tell you! In the next chapter, we'll learn a couple of new licks which will be more comfortable to play if we use this fingering.

E chord positions

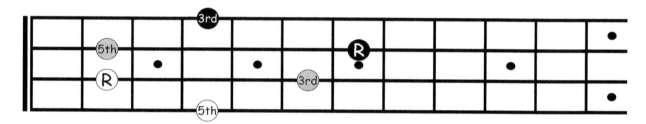

Maybe you already guessed what's coming up now. Yes, we have to move the double-stops up to the "F chord double-stop position" and the "G chord double-stop position."

F chord positions

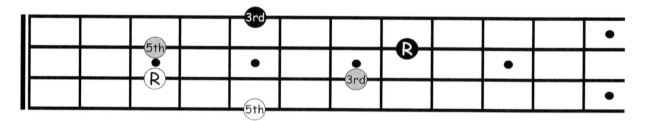

G chord positions

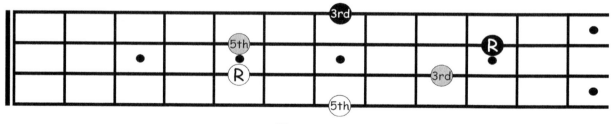

68

When you feel comfortable with the four positions we have just played, be sure that you also are able to start your lick from the low strings or from the two in the middle. The following two examples will illustrate the idea.

Structure 2:

Now it's time to learn another double-stop structure ("Structure 2"), which takes its basis from the G chord arpeggio. So– play the arpeggio, picture the structure of the double-stops and try out the lick.

Also with the "Structure 2" licks, I recommend that you try playing the first double-stop (on the e and a string) using the first and the second finger instead of the second and third.

G chord positions

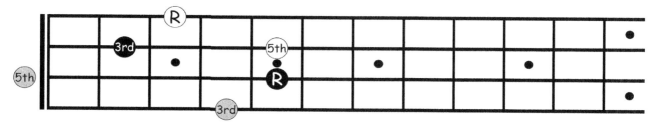

By moving the "G chord double-stop position" up the neck, we can get the A, the B♭ and the B chord double-stop positions. You might have some problems in separating the positions because of their closeness. If this is the case, then try to concentrate on the A and the B chord double-stop positions, since they are a bit farther apart. Notice that the double-stops in Structure 2 use the same positions as our "bluegrass chop chords," which we use for the G, A, B♭, and B chords.

A chord positions

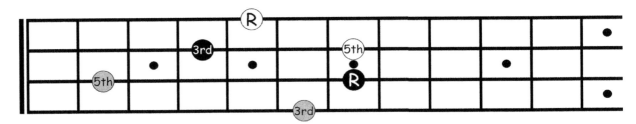

B♭ chord positions

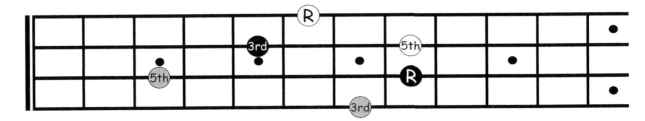

B chord positions

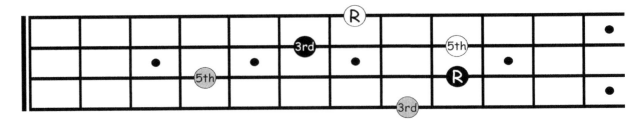

Structure 3:

The last structure takes its basic shape from the B♭-major arpeggio. One again, play the arpeggio and picture the structure of the double-stops.

B♭-major arpeggio

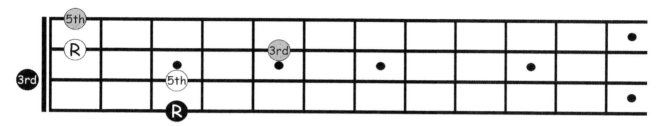

B♭ chord positions

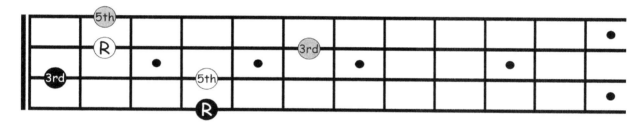

The "up-the-neck" positions which we'll play are the B, the C, the D, and the E chord double-stop positions. Also here, we're using the same positions as the (B), C, D, E bluegrass chop chords. This might be a big help in memorization.

B chord positions

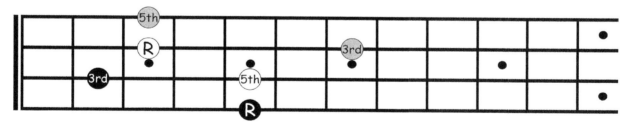

C chord positions

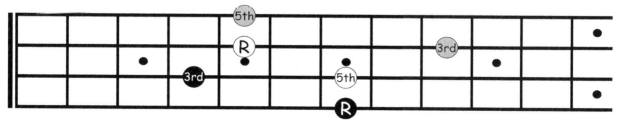

D chord positions

E chord positions

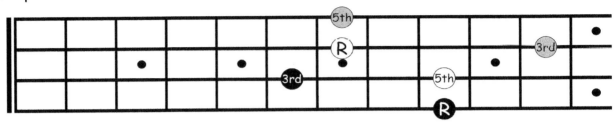

And, as a very last thing, I have to show you two chords positions which also could be used. As you will recognize, we won't use any low-string double-stops. For these two chord positions, it's not possible to go lower than the two strings in the middle. Check out the position for the "A chord double-stop position" (Structure 3) and the "F chord double-stop position" (Structure 2).

A chord positions

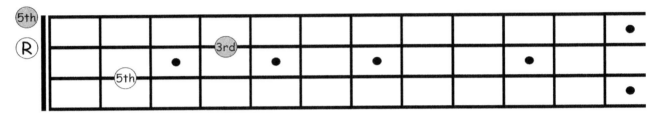

F chord positions

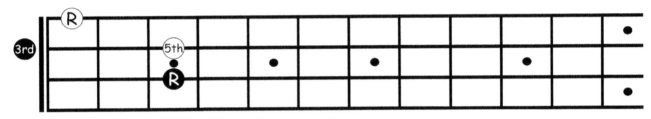

So, now you know the structures of the double-stops and the many different positions to play. Luckily, it's not necessary to know all of the positions at once. But we have to start working on how to put the three structures together. The theme double-stops is a very comprehensive subject and it's extremely important not to move too fast. I've made this mistake with a couple of my students, which made their hair turn grey a little bit too fast.

Slides:

The use of slides could make the lick sound more interesting. But! (and this is very important) – when you make the slides, then use the same fingering as when you grab the double-stops normally. This way you're avoiding uncomfortable stretches between the fingers. In the following examples two kind of slides are demonstrated, a fast one in the first line and a slow one in the second line. The last variation will also be used in the upcoming examples.

72

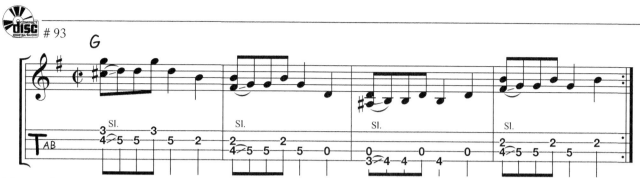

Mixing the structures:

When you start to mix up our three structures, it's recommended not to concentrate on more than three different chords. Start out with one or two keys and try to learn those areas by heart. I'll give you two examples of how this could be done. The first one is played down the neck and the second one up the neck. If you're a little insecure about the positions up the neck, then concentrate on the first example to start with, and then work on the second.

Solo 1

73

Solo 2

ASSIGNMENTS

1. Use the material just covered on two key-related chords (for example G and D or C and G, etc.).

2. Play back and forth between the chords using the double-stop licks (each lick for four bars).
   Start your licks on the two high strings.

3. Repeat the exercise, but start your licks on the two low strings.

4. Did it work ? O.K. – then try to start on the two strings in the middle.

5. Add a third chord to the exercise.

6. Pick out a tune in which you would like to try out some double-stops.

7. Try to use some slides on the double-stop licks.

74

In this chapter I'll demonstrate how to "play around" the double-stops we have just learned. To "play around" basically means to add some passing tones to our double-stops in order to give them a more interesting sound. The material that I've used for the passing tones is picked from pentatonic scales or is taken from our collection of "spices."

If you analyzed the three structures in the previous chapter, you might have recognized that only three types of double-stops are used. You might also have recognized that the movements between the double-stops repeated themselves. If not, the following overview will make the system of the movements more clear to you.

Movement 1:
Structure 2 (A-major)

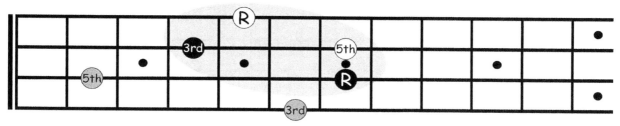

Structure 3 (C-major)

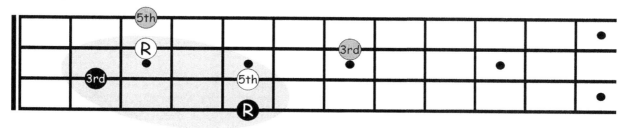

Movement 2:
Structure 1 (E-major)

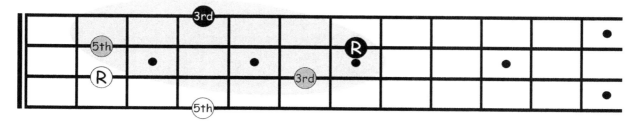

Structure 2 (A-major)

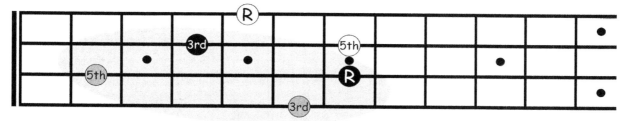

Movement 3:
Structure 3 (B-major)

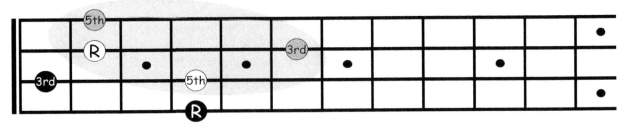

Structure 1 (E-major)

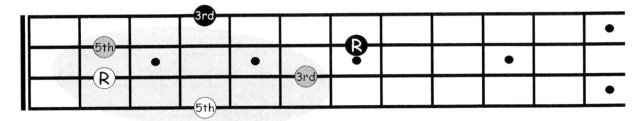

As you can see, we had three different kind of movements (1-3). So, if we are able to "play around" those three different movements, it won't take us long before we'll be able to play in and out of the structures in a tasteful way.

I have composed a couple of licks, in which we'll "play around" the double-stops. For each movement, pick out two licks you would like to use in improvising (one moving down and one moving up). The licks are of varying difficulty, so pick out some licks that fit your level. But before we start, I have to show you a common technique used with double-stops: the "picked slide." The idea is to continue picking the string even though we have a slide. In order to get the right feeling/sound, try to play the picked slide with a kind of loose touch.

 # 96

And now it's time for collecting ideas for your "bag of licks."

Movement 1 (C-major):

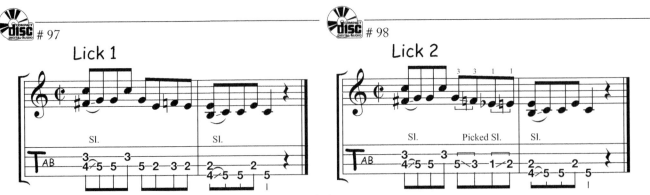

76

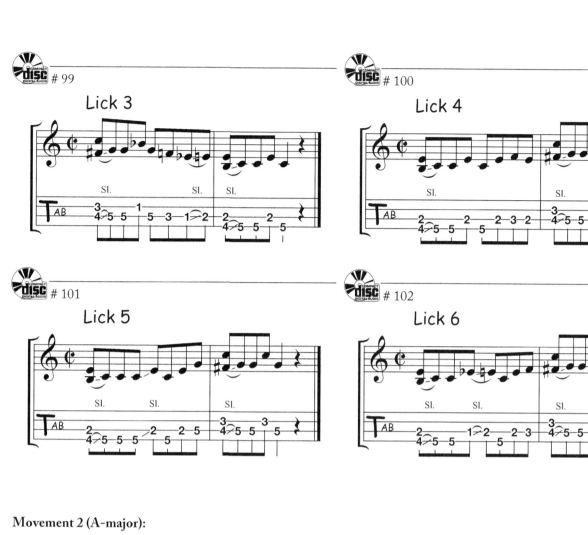

Movement 2 (A-major):

77

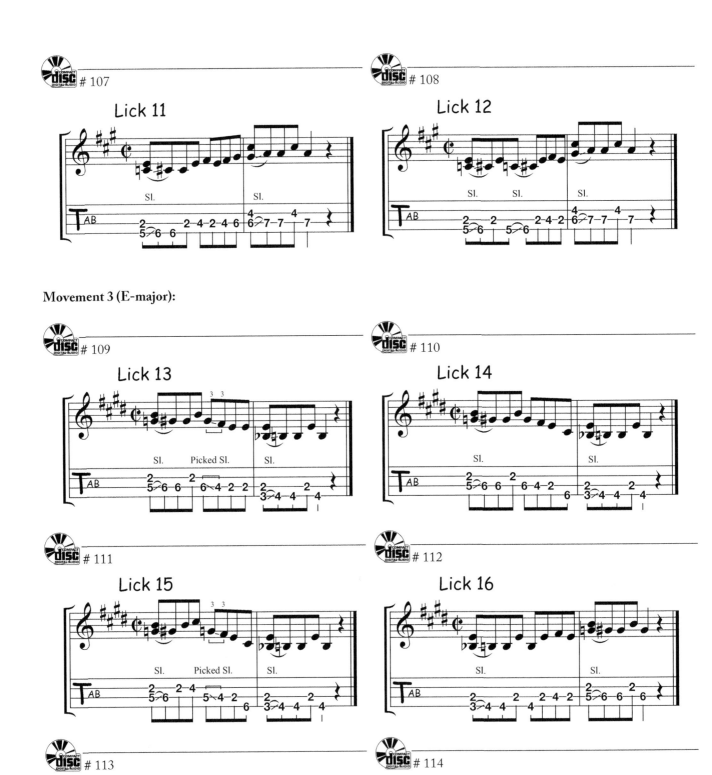

Movement 3 (E-major):

The next step would be to put the licks into the structures (1-3) from Chapter 17. As you can see, it's quite easy to come out with some really interesting lines to use for improvising.

78

Structure 1 (E-major)

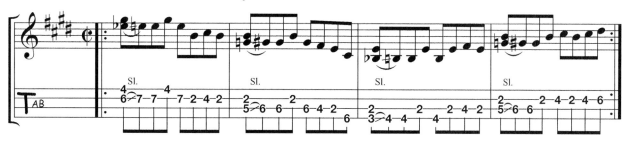

Structure 2 (A-major)

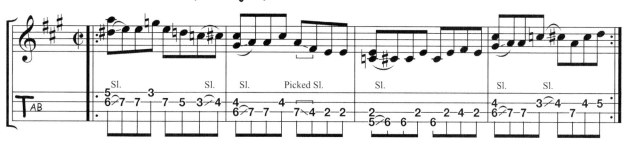

Structure 3 (B-major)

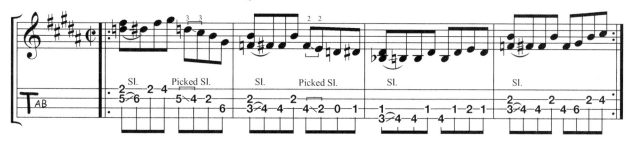

In the following example I'll show you what a ("playing around" with double-stops) solo could sound like. In the second line I chose to stay a while on the E double-stop in order to give myself a small break. And in the last line of the solo, I apply the system of "coming home" (see Chapter 12) by using a double-stop containing the root of the chord.

Solo

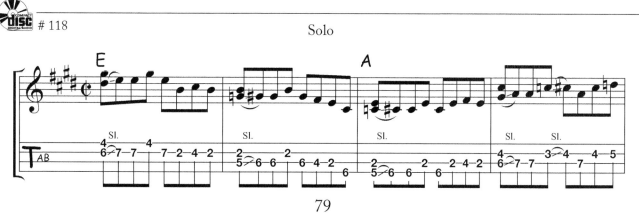

The ghost note:

The licks that you have learned in this chapter might work best on tunes in a medium or medium/fast tempo. If you have to improvise on a very fast tune, you might have to "play around" less and keep it simple. Another technique to use on fast tunes is the "ghost note technique." Instead of playing the last note of a double-stop lick, a muted string is picked. The muting is done by slightly touching the string with one of the fingers of the left hand, while moving from one position to another. The ghost note is indicated with an (x) in the following example.

119

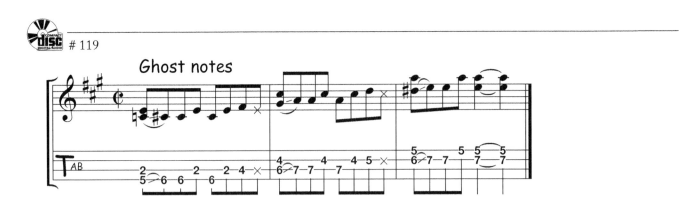

Variations on the picked slide:

In the last examples I'll show you a couple of common variations on the picked slide. Where or how to use the variations depends on what sound you want to create. As you'll hear, the variations with the picked slides come out more bluesy.

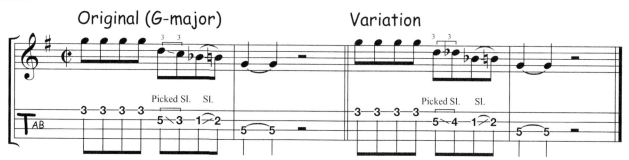

Original (G-major)   Variation

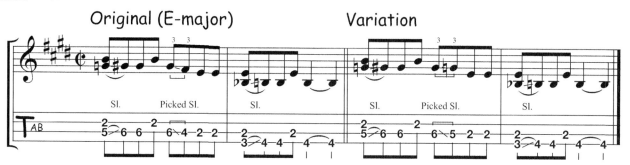

Original (E-major)   Variation

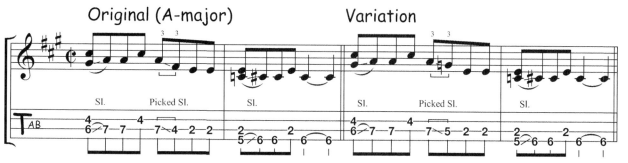

Original (A-major)   Variation

ASSIGNMENTS

1. Use your favorite double-stop licks to build some lines on structure 1 (E-major), structure 2 (A-major) and structure 3 (B-major).

2. Try to improvise a while with the following chord progression.

‖ E | E | B | B ‖

3. Now try to improvise with this chord progression.

‖ A | A | E | E ‖

4. In the following chord progression you can mix up your ideas.

5. Try to transpose structure 3 (B-major) three frets up the neck (D-major) and use your licks in this position.

6. The last assignment will use a chord progression in the key of A-major for improvising. The advanced picker should also transpose the whole chord progression up a half tone, (into the key of B♭-major) for a further improvisation challenge.

7. In Chapter 17, we also had some double-stops using open strings. Be aware of the fact that not all of the licks we just played will fit double-stops using open strings. Figure out which licks will work and which won't.

8. Try to compose a couple of double-stops licks. (You don't have to start the lick with a slide, the way I've done it in the chapter). Make up one or two exercises in which you can use your licks.

CHAPTER 19: Other Double-Stop Ideas

The last two chapters can give the foundation of double-stop playing. So, if you have learned your lessons well, you're ready to move on.

Connecting the structures:

As we were learning the three different structures, you might have recognized that both structures 2 and 3, contained the B and the B♭ chord. Similarly, structures 1 and 3 contain the D and the E chord. Actually, all of the three structures could be used for any major chord double-stop you want to play. You just have to figure out the position (up the neck). I'll give you an example to play in which the double-stops for the D and the G chord are used. As you can see, we need to move up the neck quite a bit to arrive at the last structure. The numbers 1-3 refer to the numbers of the three different structures (see Chapter 17).

D-major structures:

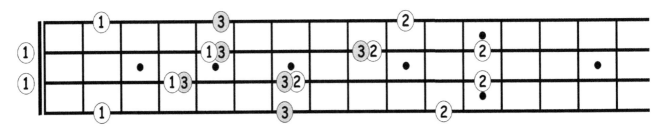

G-major structures:

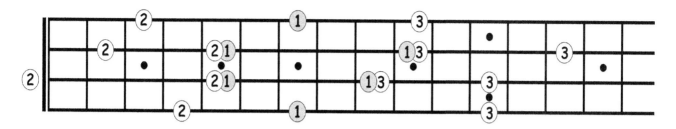

I think that two positions for each chord should be enough to cover our needs for variety. You just have to learn how to move from one structure to another and you'll soon be conquering your fingerboard. Check out the following three possibilities.

123

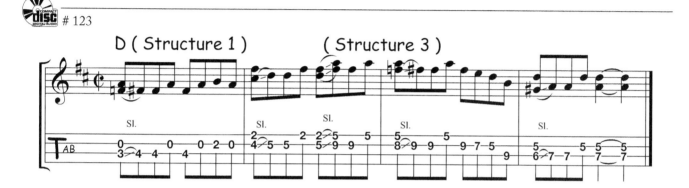

124

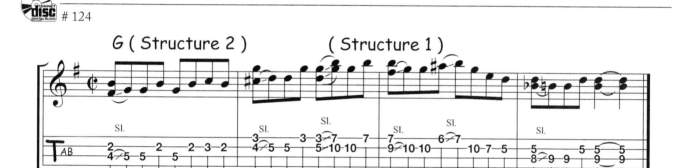

125

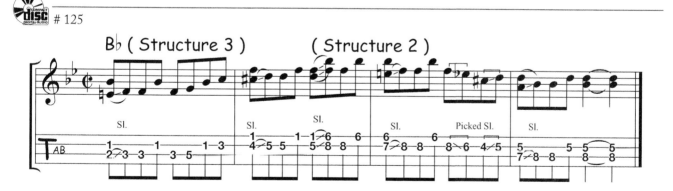

Other double-stops shapes:

In order to simplify the learning and the picturing of the double-stops in Chapter 17, we reduced the number of double-stop shapes down to three different shapes. Now it's time to look at the other ones, which in the case of

D chord (see Chapter 17) would give us the following three shapes.

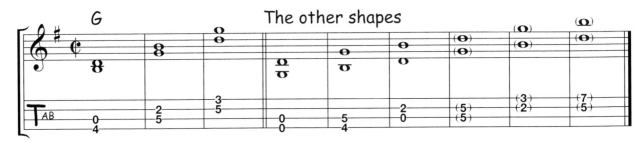

All of the three new shapes can be found in the same positions as the three structures we have already learned. Take a look at the two next examples in which all double-stop possibilities are written out for the chords G and B♭.

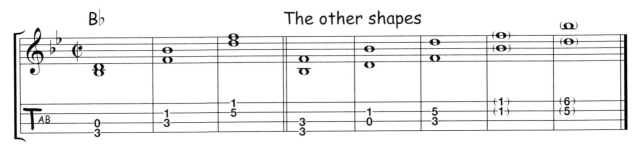

Our new shapes could be mixed, without any problems, with some of the ideas that we already have learned. To illustrate this, I've written out a couple of examples to play.

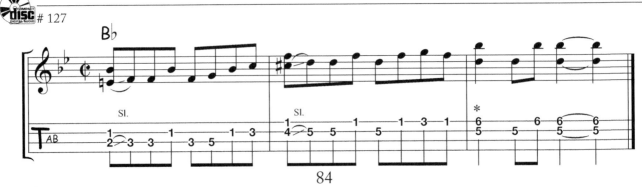

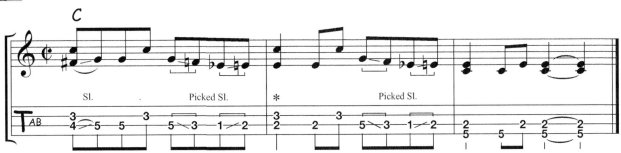

Chord numbers:

In order to be able to explain some of the upcoming material, I have to be sure that you know the system of the chord numbers. As you might remember, the C-major scale is a scale containing seven different tones (see Chapter 1). If we name the tones of the scale from one to seven, each tone will get the following number:

c - 1   d - 2   e - 3   f - 4   g - 5   a - 6   b - 7

Like the tones of the scale, we could also give the chords the same numbers. The C chord (in the key of C-major) would be called the "one chord." The F chord would be the "four chord" and the G chord would be the "five chord." For the chord numbering, it's standard to use the Roman numeral notation. So would the "one chord" be written out like this: (I). Check out the following chords (in the key of C-major) and their numbers:

F = (IV)   G = (V)   G7 = (V7)   Am = (VI m)   Dm = (II m)   D = (II)

In a major key, the most common chords would be the (I), the (IV) and the (V) chord. With this knowledge it's quite easy to figure out the I, IV and V chord in any key. You just have to know the major-scale of the key. In the key of G-major, the (I) = G, the (IV) = C and the (V) = D. Agree? (In the appendix you'll find a overview of all major-scales.)

I think this should be enough theory for now. Keep it in mind and let's continue with some more double-stop ideas.

Harmonizing the major scale:

Harmonizing a major scale by adding harmony notes to it (building double-stops) is another useful technique to use. The first step would be to choose a major scale which we'd like to harmonize. Let us use the G-major scale. The second step would be to choose an interval to use for harmonizing. The most commonly-used intervals (in bluegrass) are 3rds or 6ths. In the following examples we'll first play the G-major scale plain and then harmonized in double-stops. The intervals will be minor and major 6ths. Notice that all of the tones in the double-stops belong to the key of G-major.

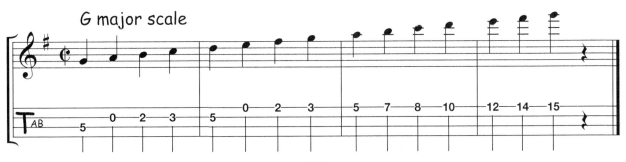

85

Harmonized in 6ths

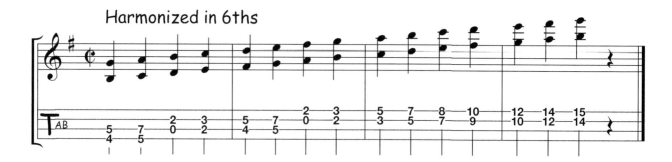

In the following box system, we'll take a look at the scale in one octave. As you can see, I've written out which double-stop belongs to each chord (G, C and D). For each chord, we have two double-stops, one containing the major 3rd and the root and the other one containing the perfect 5th and the major 3rd. I've also added an example to play in which you'll hear the sound of these double-stops.

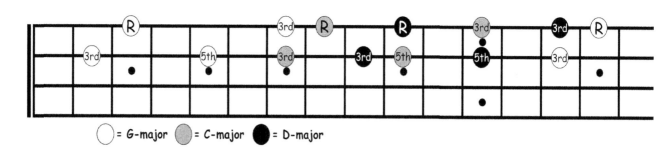

◯ = G-major   ◐ = C-major   ● = D-major

129

Major scale movements:

The harmonized major scale is really good if you want to compose some movements going up or down the neck. The idea is to use some of the double-stops as "passing double-stops" as the following example will illustrate. Notice that all of these movements can be played using only your first and second finger.

130

Notice that the movement on the C chord (IV) was slightly different than what we did on the G (I) and the D chord (V).

The system of "passing double-stops" could also be used when we have to move from one chord to another. Use your ear when you have to compose some "major-scale movement licks." I've written out some moves to play in the key of G-major.

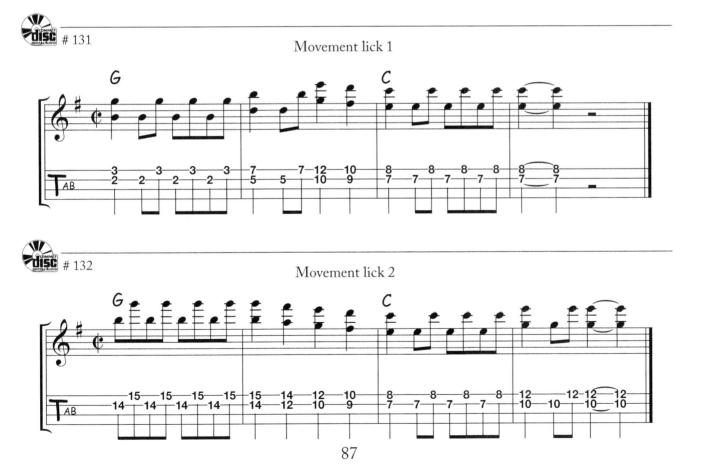

87

133

Movement lick 3

134

Movement lick 4

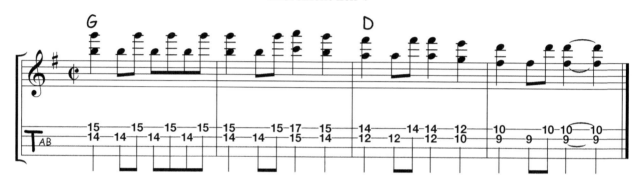

135

Movement lick 5

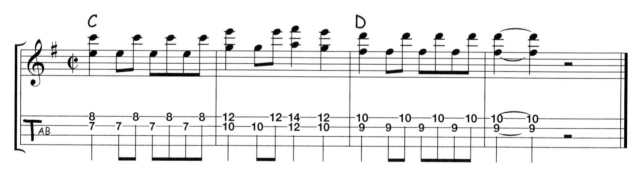

136

Movement lick 6

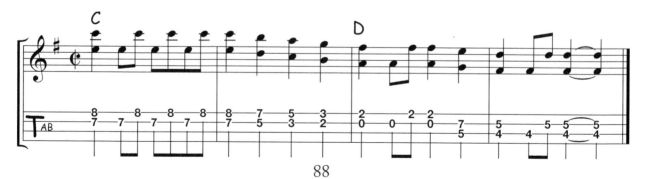

137

Movement lick 7

138

Movement lick 8

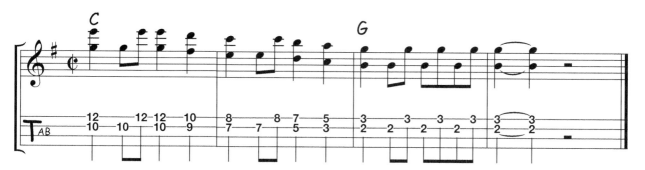

139

Movement lick 9

140

Movement lick 10

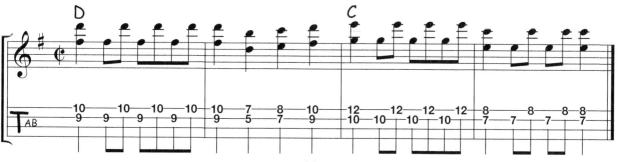

Movement lick 11

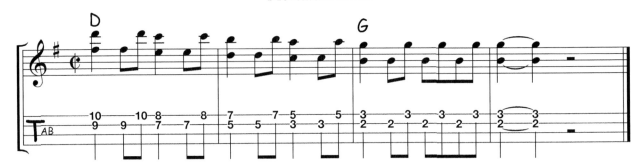

Movement lick 12

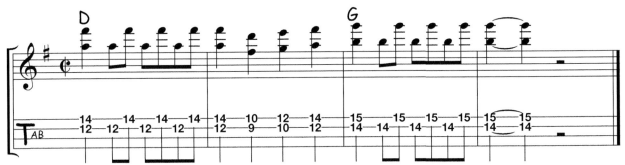

All of the movements could naturally also be played one octave lower, as you can hear in this next solo. It's recommended to use more than your first and second finger, for these kind of "down-the-neck" movements. Fingering suggestions are added in the standard notation.

Solo 1

Harmonizing in 3rds:

As we were harmonizing in 6ths, we actually took the G-major scale and added another tone to each tone, a major or a minor 6th below. By harmonizing in 3rds, we have to add a major or a minor 3rd to the major scale. But this time above each tone. So, once again it's time to play the G-major scale plain and then harmonized in 3rds.

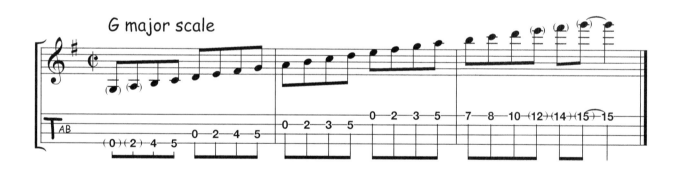

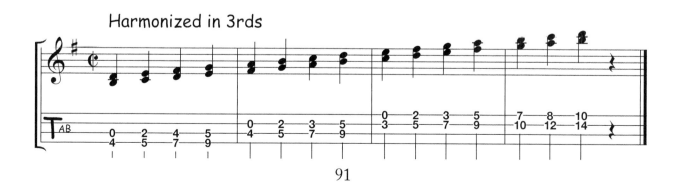

As you might have recognized, the double-stops in the G-major scale actually came out with the same two tones, no matter if we used a 6th below or a 3rd above. The 6th below the g tone would give us the tone b, but the 3rd above the g tone would also come out as a b tone.

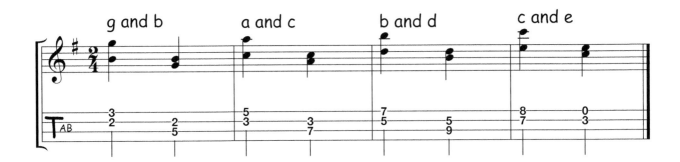

So, every movement which we already have played in 6ths, could also be played in 3rds.

Played in 6ths

Played in 3rds

Both intervals can, of course, be used within the same solo, as is shown in the following example:

By harmonizing the major scale in 6ths and 3rds, the major scale was used for the first time as a source for building some interesting melodic double-stop lines. The key and the melodic movements stayed in front and the double-stops, containing the chord tones, were often used as a place to start our lines. If you practice the harmonized major scale so well that you can play some good-sounding melodic lines on the spot, you might also be able to improvise in tunes without knowing the chord progression by heart. Your ear is showing you the way. Notice that major-scale movements don't give a bluesy sound. So if you have to improvise on a bluesy-sounding tune, it's recommended to avoid major-scale movements, or to mix them up with some more bluesy ideas.

Chord-related movements:

Instead of using the key (of the song) as the source, it's obvious that the chords could also be used for building double-stop movements. When doing this, it's important to find some double-stop movements which could fit any major chord. The chord-related movements are much more limited, in relation to the harmonized major scale, but really good if you like to improvise on a tune, without paying so much attention to what key you are in. The chords of the tune will guide you.

93

Take a look at this next example which is quite similar to Ex. 130. As you can see, the G chord movement is transposed to the C and the D chord.

If we compare this example with Ex. 130, we'll see that the G and the D chord stayed the same, but the C chord had a small change in the "passing double-stop." We could say that the C chord (IV chord) has two different kinds of sounds. A "major scale" related sound and a "moveable chord" related sound. What sound do you prefer? The subject, "the IV chord" will also be covered in Chapter 26 (Other Spices).

Check out the next example in which only chord related movements are used. For some of the double-stops, a small slide coming from one fret below is used. This kind of "one-fret-below slide" is often used as an interesting approach to double-stops.

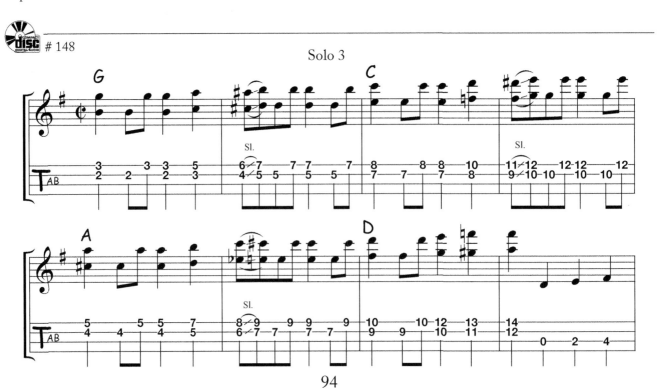

The minor 7th sound:

In Chapter 9 (The Spices) we learned about how the ♭7 added to the pentatonic-scale would give us a kind of bluesy sound. So, if we want to make our double-stops more bluesy sounding, we could actually do the same thing here. The best sounding double-stops are those combining the ♭7 with the major 3rd or the perfect 5th.

G7 arpeggio

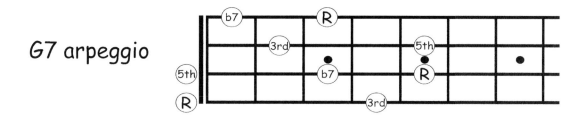

I've written out a couple of bluesy sounding double-stop licks to play. As you can see, I've also marked the minor 7th spots, with the ♭7 sign. In the second example I used a common chromatic movement going from the root down to the ♭7. (The subject chromatic will be covered in Chapter 26 – Other Spices).

149

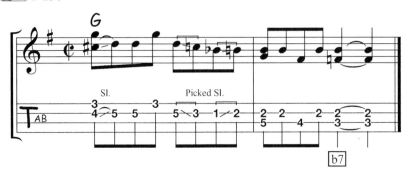

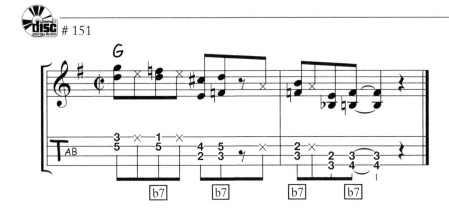

Beyond the bluesy sound, the ♭7 can also be used at the end of a line, to give a leading effect. This works very well going from the (V) chord to the (I) chord, but also from the (I) chord to the (IV) chord, as the next examples illustrate.

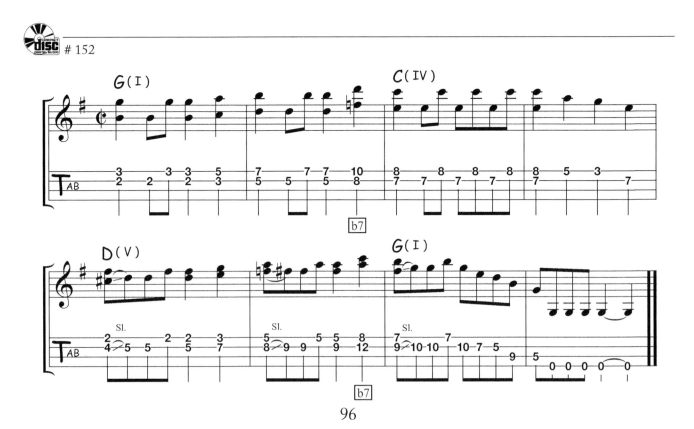

153

The major 6th sound:

This first example will show you a quite commonly-used trick, which implies the major 6th and the root together in a double-stop. In this situation the major 6th is used as a kind of an outside tone which then is resolved into a perfect 5th. – Great sound !

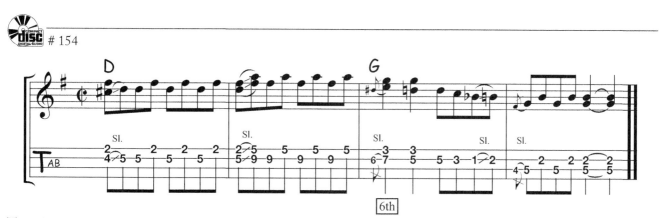

154

The 6th can also be used inside a double-stop lick in order to give us a more jazzy sound.

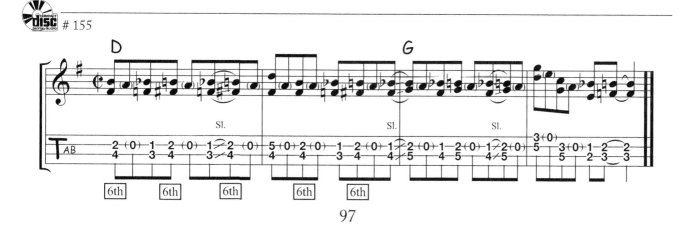

155

Other techniques to use:

If you want to improvise a solo in a bluegrass waltz (¾ time), it's quite helpful to use double-stops played with tremolo. This technique could also be used by "active backup" (quiet solo playing behind the lead singing part). Check out the use of tremolo in ¾ time.

Another technique to use with a bluegrass waltz would be, what I call, the "banjo waltz technique." It's a banjo technique that mandolin pickers also use. As you can see, the use of "major-scale movements" and "chord-related movements" are indispensable for this technique.

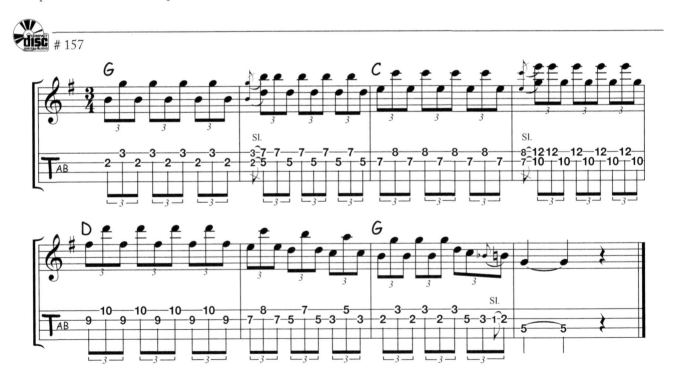

Naturally, we could also use tremolo on standard four-beat bluegrass tunes. Slow tunes are especially well suited to this, combining double-stops and tremolo playing. Similar to the "banjo waltz technique" in ¾ time, cross-picking is another interesting technique to use on four-beat tunes. (The theme cross-picking will be discussed separately in Chapter 24)

ASSIGNMENTS

1. Try to use the system of "connecting the structures," on a tune or chord progression familiar to you.

2. Be sure you know the "numbers of the chords." Which one of the following assertions is wrong ?

    F = (IV) chord in C-major
    E = (V) chord in A-major
    Em = (VI m) chord in G-major
    G = (III) chord in D-major
    E♭ = (IV) chord in B♭-major

3. Harmonize the D-major scale with the use of double-stops.

4. Compose some "major-scale movements" in the key of D-major.

5. Play some of the "chord-related movements" you have learned with a tune in A-major.

6. Pick out a bluegrass waltz to use for double-stop/tremolo playing.

CHAPTER 20: Minor Chords

In this chapter we'll learn about how to treat minor chords appearing in major keys. The two most common minor chords in the key of G-major are Em and Am. If we're using the system of "the chord numbers" (see Chapter 19), The Am is the (II m) chord and the Em is the (VI m) chord. In order to figure out what scales to use, we need to use the G-major scale as a basis.

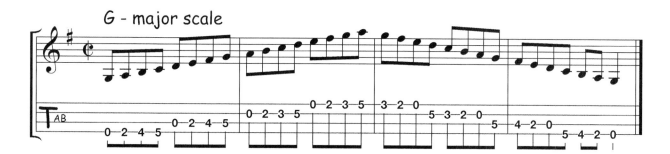

Let's play the G-major scale once again, but instead of starting on the g tone, we'll start on the a tone. This new scale is called the dorian scale. The A dorian scale is a scale that has a "minor sound" and it's a scale to use with the Am chord (in the key of G-major). Play the A dorian scale and listen to its sound.

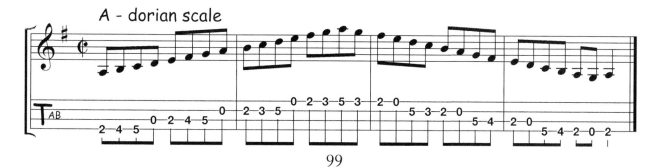

And now, let's play the G-major scale, starting on the e tone. This scale would be the E-minor scale. The minor and the dorian scale are both scales that have a "minor sound." Now play the E-minor scale and listen to its sound.

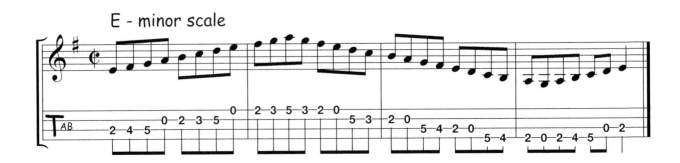

Some of you might ask yourself if it's really necessary to learn two new scales for each key in which a minor chord appears. –The answer is no ! The fact that the three scales just played contain the same tone material, makes it obvious that the main key could guide us through the minor chords. An Am chord will be played, but we will be thinking G-major scale. The following solo (in the key of G-major) contains Am and Em chords. Try to keep the structure of the G-major scale in mind while playing the minor chord passages. In order to keep the solo melodic, I started all of the "minor-chord lines" on a chord-tone (mostly the root of the minor chord). On the major chords, material we have already learned is used.

 # 158

Solo 1

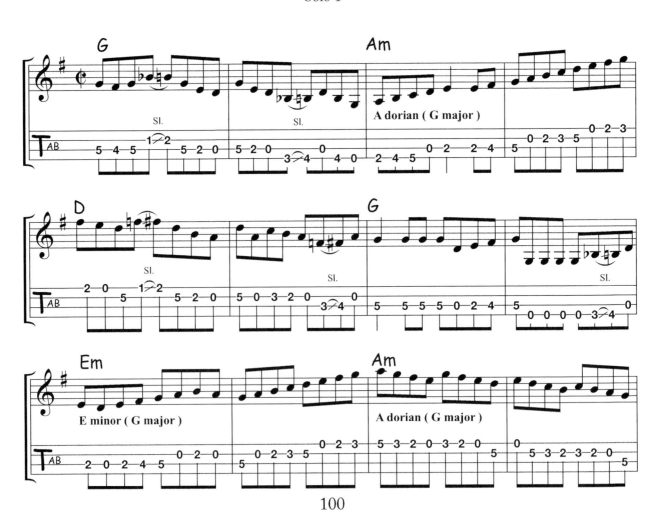

100

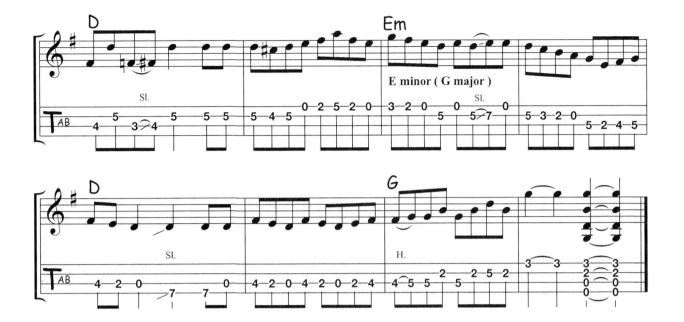

When we're improvising on the dorian or the minor scale, we need to use our ears much more than we did when we were learning the pentatonic scales. Each of the "minor scales" contains seven tones to improvise on. Three of these seven tones would be the chord tones of the minor chord. The other four are tones in which you shouldn't stay for a long time– use these four tones as passing tones, going from one chord tone to another. It's recommended that you learn the chord-tones of the minor chords, but not a must. As I've already said, your ears will tell you on which tones to rest and which to use as passing tones. The best way to obtain a good melodic line is to avoid big intervals– just keep it simple by playing small melodic movements, the same way as done in the solo just played.

Dorian scale contra minor scale:

Some of you might like to know the difference between the dorian and the minor scale. The best way to illustrate this is by looking at how to treat an Am chord in two different keys (G and C-major). We already know that the Am chord is the (II m) chord in the key of G-major, and that the associated scale would be dorian. In C-major, the Am chord would be the (VI m) chord, on which we need to play a minor scale. Check out the two scales and their sound.

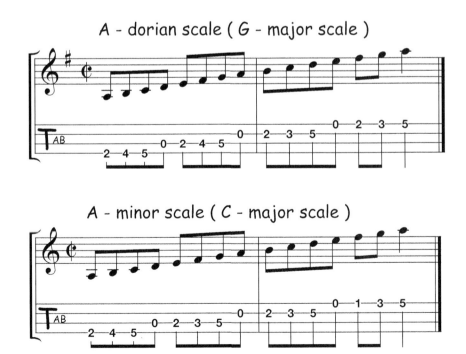

101

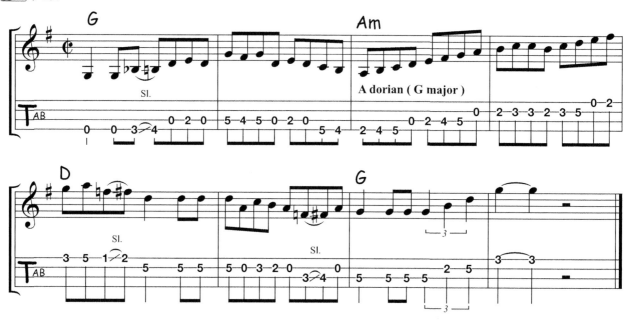

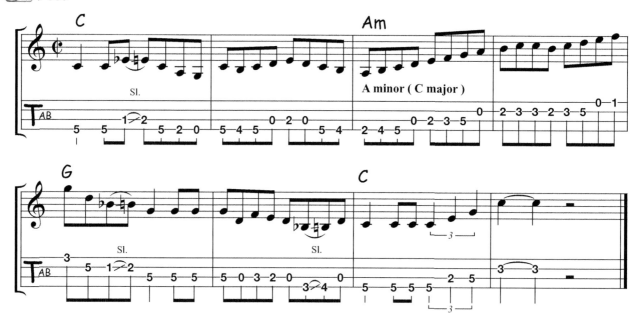

If we are counting the tones in both of the scales, we'll see that it's the sixth tone that makes the difference. The dorian scale has a major 6th and the minor scale has a minor 6th.

Let's make it easy:

The fact that improvising is quite often used in situations where we don't have much time for analyzing could make the choice: "dorian scale or minor scale" a problem. Some of you might also find it too confusing to use the main key as a substitution for our "minor chord" scales. And what about, how to collect minor chord licks for our "bag of licks"? Do we really need to have some dorian licks and some minor licks? The solution to our problems would be to compose some licks which would be playable in both dorian and minor situations. The fact that it's the sixth tone which makes the difference between the dorian and the minor scale could be a big help for us. What about using only one scale in which we'll leave out the sixth tone– **a minor (no 6th) scale?** Listen to the scale and play the examples.

102

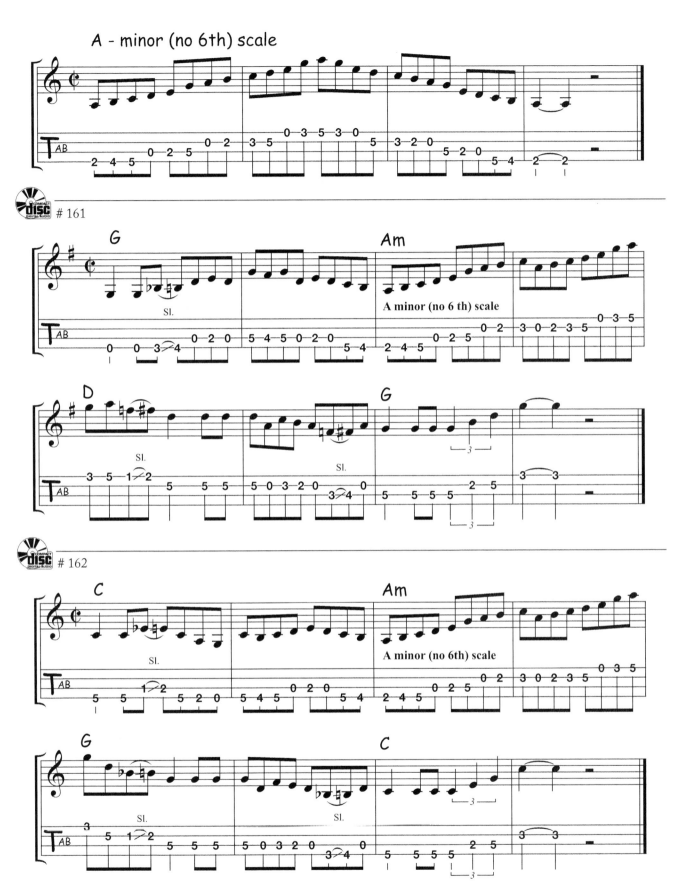

As you can see, we just made everything much more clear and easy to understand. One chord - one scale. The minor (no 6th) scale could, of course, also be called the dorian (no 6th) scale. I chose to use the first name because of the fact that the minor scale is generally more well-known. In the following solo (in the key of G-major) I also used the minor (no 6th) scale with the Em chord. For further study, other minor (no 6th) scales can also be found in the appendix.

Solo 2

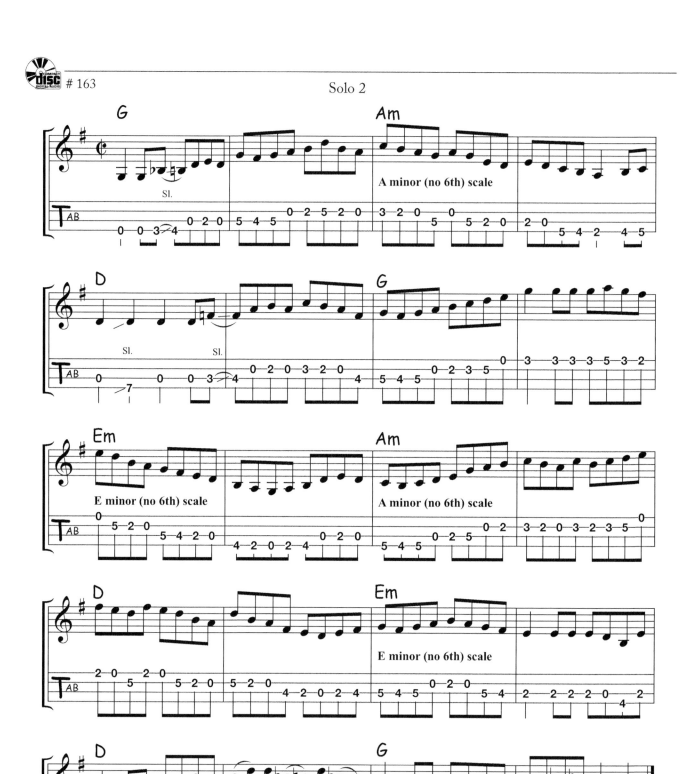

The (III m) chord:

According to the "chord numbers," the third chord (in the key of G-major) would be the B chord or the Bm chord. Although the (II m) chord and the (VI m) chord would be the most common minor chords (in major keys), it could also happen that a (III m) chord sometimes appears. By playing the G-major scale, starting on the b tone, we'll get the scale to play on the Bm (III m) chord– The phrygian scale.

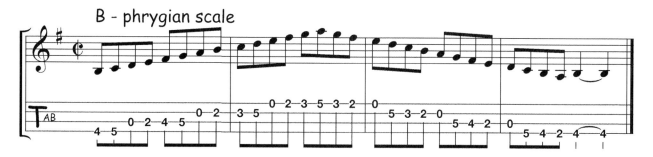

Check out the following two solos in which the phrygian scale as opposed to the minor (no 6th) scale is used. Although the phrygian scale would be the most correct scale to use (with improvisation over a (III m) chord), I think that the minor (no 6th) scale would work out just as well in an improvising situation. What do you think ?

164

Solo 3

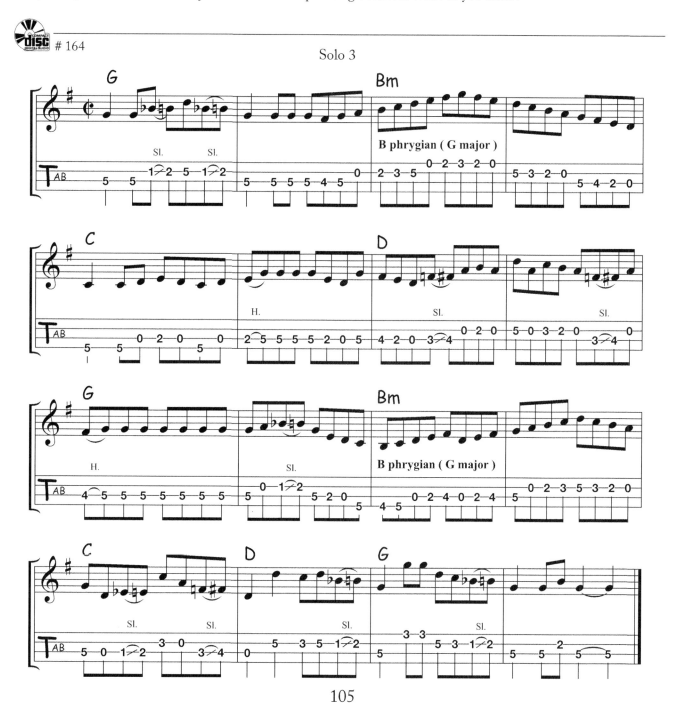

The (IV m) chord:

When a (IV m) chord appears in a chord progression, it's nearly always as in the following example, where a major (IV) chord is turned into a minor (IV m) chord.

|| G | G7 | C (IV) | Cm (IVm) |
| G | D | G | G ||

A common technique to use on these (IV) → (IV m) chord changes, is to convert the major chord lick into a minor chord lick. The system is quite simple. At first we'll play a pentatonic lick on the C chord, and then we'll play precisely the same lick on the minor chord– but every major 3rd in the lick has to be changed into a minor 3rd. A variation on the

106

minor chord also sounds good. The minor (no 6th) and the dorian scale could also be used on the (IV m) chord. The following examples should explain the idea.

166

167

168

169

ASSIGNMENTS

1. Pick out a tune in which one or more minor chords appear.

2. Try to figure out the "numbers" of the minor chords (IIm, IIIm, IVm, or VIm).

107

3. Compose a couple of licks for the minor chords, using the related scale(s) or the minor (no 6th) scale.

4. Try to improvise on one of the chord progressions already used in this chapter.

CHAPTER 21: Minor Keys

At this point I think it might be a good idea to take a look at how to treat tunes in minor keys. The fact that around 95% or more of all vocal bluegrass tunes are written in a major key led me to choose to concentrate this one chapter on minor keys. In contrast to vocal tunes, we have a lot of minor key instrumentals in bluegrass music. If you try to think about all of the minor key instrumentals you know, you'll recognize that all of these tunes have a really strong melody. I would even dare to come out with the assertion that minor key tunes in general are more melodic than major key tunes. Melodic playing is also the key word when we are talking improvisation in minor keys.

Before hitting the road into the land of the minor keys, let's take a look at our "means of transport": the minor scale.

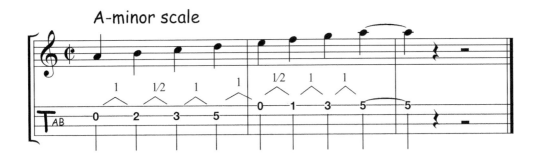

In the previous chapter we've already played the A-minor scale as a scale to use with the Am chord (VI chord) in the key of C-major. In this chapter, the minor scale will be used in a slightly different way, as part of a new technique called horizontal playing.

Vertical as opposed to horizontal playing:

Nearly everything that we've been playing until now, could be put into the category of vertical playing. When each chord in a chord progression is treated separately, by using another scale with each chord, we're talking vertical playing. In horizontal playing, we're only using one scale the whole way through our improvisation. Horizontal playing does not work that well on major key bluegrass tunes, with the small exception of bluesy bluegrass tunes (see the next chapter – The Blues Scale), but in a tune in a minor key this kind of playing works very well.

Horizontal playing:

If we want to use horizontal playing with a tune in the key of A-minor, we need to use the A-minor scale the whole way through our improvisation. In horizontal playing it's really not necessary to pay any heed to the chord changes of the tune, our ears and what we hear will guide us through our solo.

Horizontal playing only works if we are playing melodically. We need to play an improvised melody using the minor scale. In order to show you what I mean when I say melodic playing, I've written out a small example to play. As you can see, I'm only playing up and down the A-minor scale, creating melodic lines. Try to repeat the exercise for a while. When you feel confident with this kind of melodic up and down scale movement, then try to go on playing some other melodic ideas. You don't have to use eighth notes only. The most important thing is to keep the lines moving on and to avoid the use of big intervals.

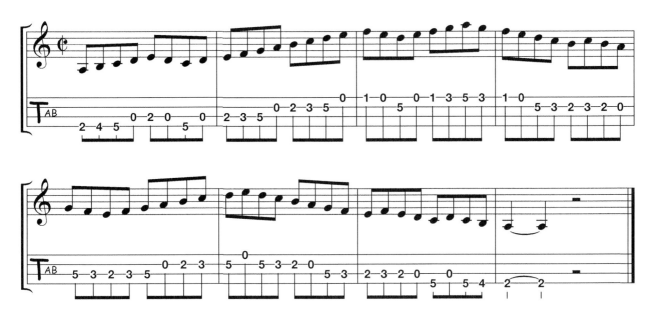

The next step would be to try out this kind of melodic playing with a chord progression in the key of A-minor. In order to make the beginning of your improvisation sound right, start your solo on the root of the first chord of the chord progression. It takes some courage to start out using horizontal playing, but as you'll see, it's not that difficult to come up with some nice melodic lines. Now the big question is: "Did the lines we just played fit the chord-progression at all?" Probably not all of the time, but (and this is the great thing about horizontal playing) our lines don't have to fit the chords 100% of the time. In horizontal playing, a good-sounding melodic line is more important than the harmonic match.

Try to play the following two examples together with the CD. Listen carefully to the lines. Do they fit the chords or not?

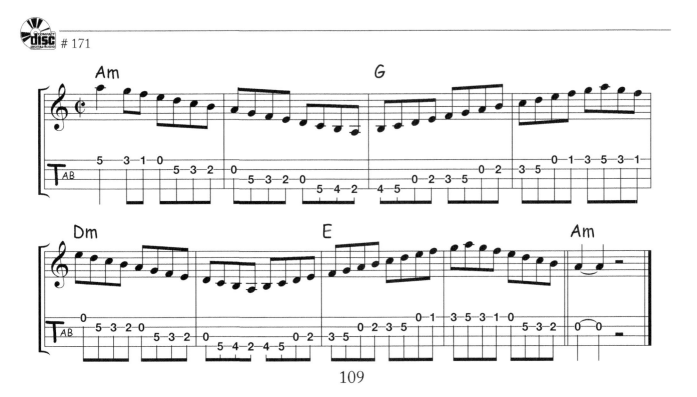

172

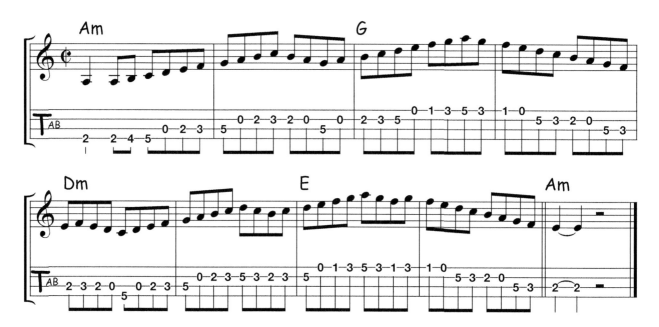

As you can hear, melodic moving lines work very well in a minor key. Even in places where the first note of the measure comes as a non-chord tone. It all works because of the melodic nature of the lines.

Symmetrical sequences:

Some other tools to use with horizontal playing are the symmetrical sequences. Symmetrical sequences are basically a group of notes which are moved symmetrically down or up the scale (did you get it?). OK! I'll let the examples show you the idea.

Group of four notes:

 # 173

Symmetrical sequence 1

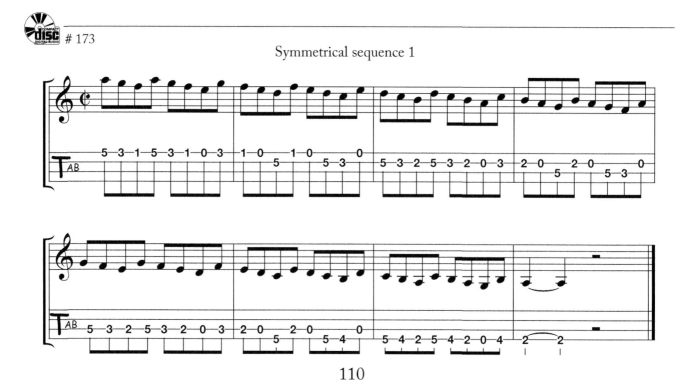

174

Symmetrical sequence 2

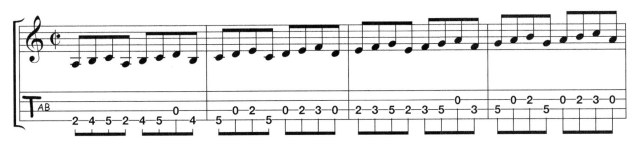

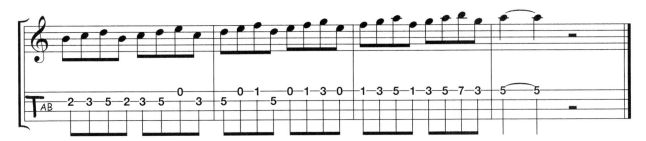

175

Symmetrical sequence 3

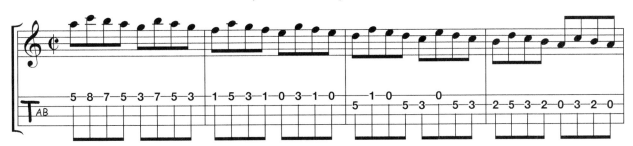

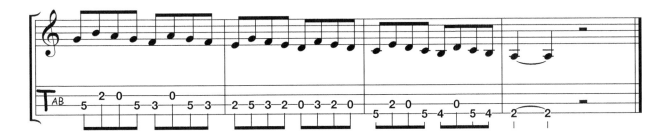

176

Symmetrical sequence 4

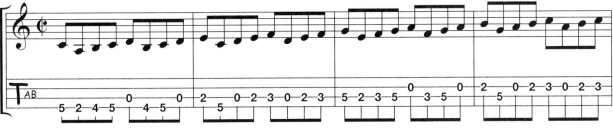

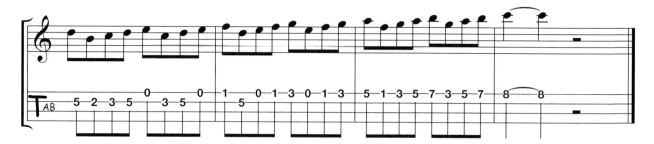

By practicing symmetrical sequences, you'll get a group of small melodic ideas to use for improvising horizontally. It's not necessary to play the sequences in their full length while improvising. Small parts mixed up with other ideas will surely come out sounding really well. Don't worry too much about where or how to use the symmetrical sequences, if you practice them, they'll automatically become a part of your playing.

The amount of ways to sequence a group of notes symmetrically is endless. Any small idea can be moved around as a symmetrical sequence. Try to come up with some ideas of your own.

Adjustable playing:

Up until now, we didn't have any problems with using horizontal playing as long as our played lines were continuous in their movement. But what should we do if we want to embellish our improvisation by adding some longer sounding tones to our playing? At first it's important to remember that not any note will work as a note to rest on. Our "resting note" has to fit the chord played at that particular moment. As already learned, we know that horizontal playing could be used without paying any attention to the chord changes. So how should we now be able to play some longer sounding tones fitting the chord changes without knowing that chord is played? No problem! Our ears will guide us at these places by using adjustable playing. By playing a longer sounding tone to rest on, without knowing what chord is played, two things can happen. Either the played tone will fit the chord or it won't. If the tone fits, it's great, but if it doesn't, we need to adjust the tone by changing it to the tone one step above or below in the scale. Most of the time this "new" tone will then fit the played chord and the rest can be done. Adjustable playing is commonly used by improvisers using horizontal playing and can even make the improvisation sound more interesting. The following examples will demonstrate the use of adjustable playing (marked a-p). In the last example a double adjustment had to be used in order to make everything fit (marked d-a).

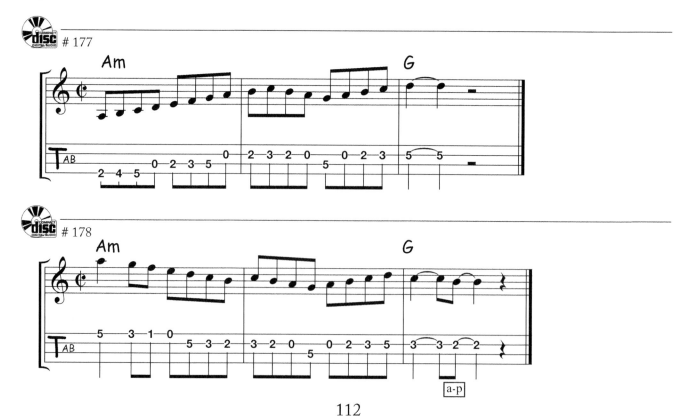

112

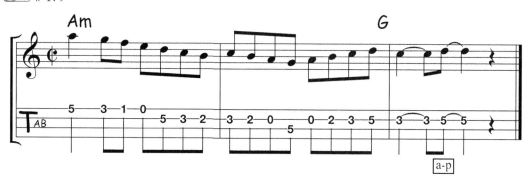

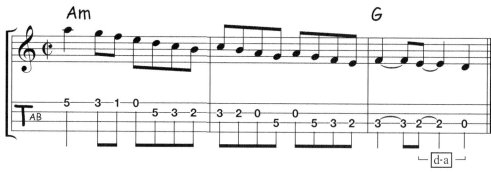

Vertical playing:

Of course vertical playing could also be used in minor keys. In order to be able to understand the following explanations, it's important that you've already read and understood the previous chapter about minor chords in major keys.

The minor chords:

In the key of A-minor the one chord would be the Am (Im), with which the A-minor scale or the minor (no 6th) scale could be used. The fourth chord in the key of A-minor would be the Dm (IVm), with which the A-minor scale starting on the d tone could be used. This scale is called the D dorian scale, but with the Dm chord, a D-minor (no 6th) scale would also work out as well. The five chords in the key of A-minor would most often be an E or E7 chord (V or V7), but it could happen that an Em chord (Vm) is used. With the Em chord (Vm) the right scale would be the phrygian scale (A-minor scale starting on the e tone), but the E-minor (no 6th) scale might also be usable in some situations, even though theoretically the phrygian scale might be the most correct one.

The major chords:

All major chords appearing in a minor key (except the V chord) can be treated as was done in any major key, using the major pentatonic scales and the already learned "spices." But, and this is important, the use of the flatted seventh ($\flat$7) does not work out well on every major chord. In the key of A-minor it's really no problem to play the $\flat$7 of the G chord, because of the fact that the $\flat$7 (the f tone) belongs to the A-major scale, contrary to the $\flat$7 of the C chord (the B$\flat$) which doesn't fit at all. If you're unsure about the use of flatted sevenths, just leave them out for now.

The V chord in a minor key:

Our problem chord in the key of A-minor is surely our E chord (the V chord). Why? The main problem is that the major pentatonic scale, which is normally used with the major chords, doesn't fit the V chord very well. The E-major pentatonic scale contains five notes of which three notes (c$\sharp$, f$\sharp$ and g$\sharp$) don't belong to the A-minor scale. Listen to the following example in order to make your own opinion about the use of the pentatonic scale (on the V chord in a minor key).

113

181

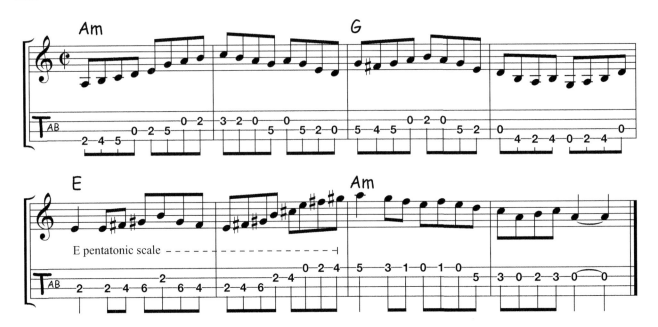

If we are looking at our E chord, we'll see that it contains the three notes: e, g♯ and b. If you then play the A-minor scale, it's obvious that the g♯ of the E chord doesn't belong to the scale. It means that playing the E chord is kind of leaving us "off key" for a moment. In order to solve our problems, we need to figure out a scale which fits both the E chord and the key (A-minor). By reading some books about jazz theory I've learned that the right solution to our problem would be the A-harmonic minor scale. This scale contains all of the three E chord tones and it stays very close to the A-minor scale by keeping six out of seven tones the same. Ok, let's listen to this scale!

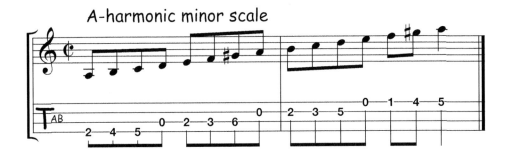

182

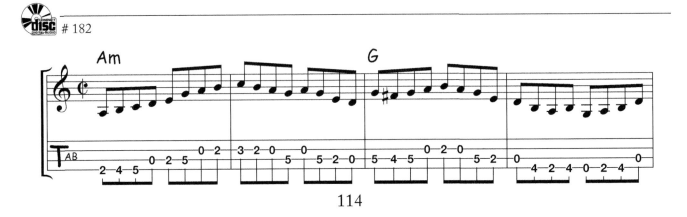

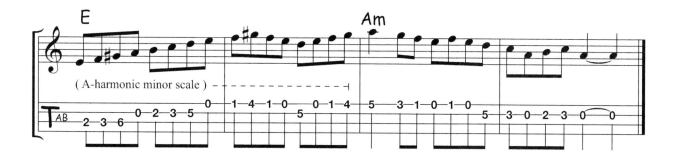

Yes! You're are probably thinking the same as I did when learning the A-harmonic minor scale. This scale just sounds too exotic for bluegrass. I knew this sound from listening to gypsy jazz and new acoustic music, but not really from straight bluegrass. The problem is the 1½ step between the f and the g♯ tone, which doesn't sound bluegrassy at all. In order to solve this problem we need to avoid moving from the f to the g♯ tone and vice versa, as demonstrated in the following examples.

183

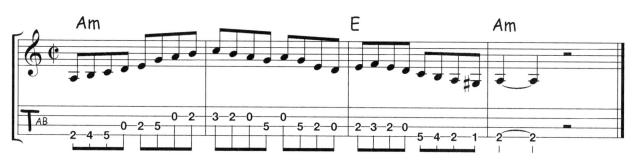

184

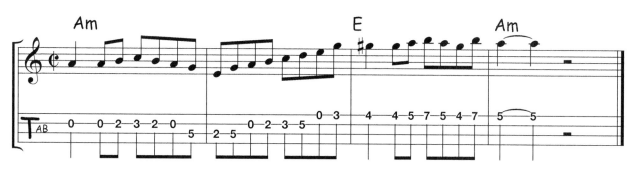

185

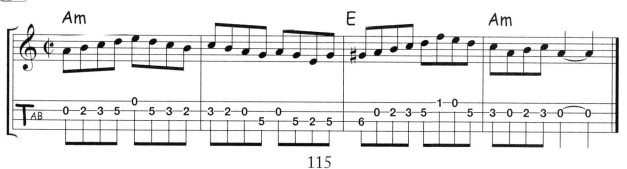

186

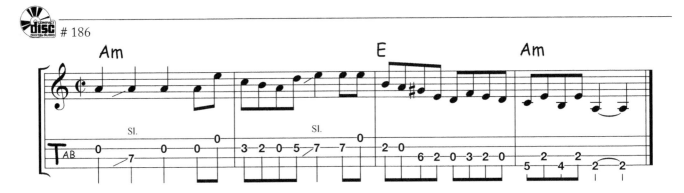

The A-harmonic minor (no 6th) scale, leaving out the f tone also works quite well with the E chord.

187

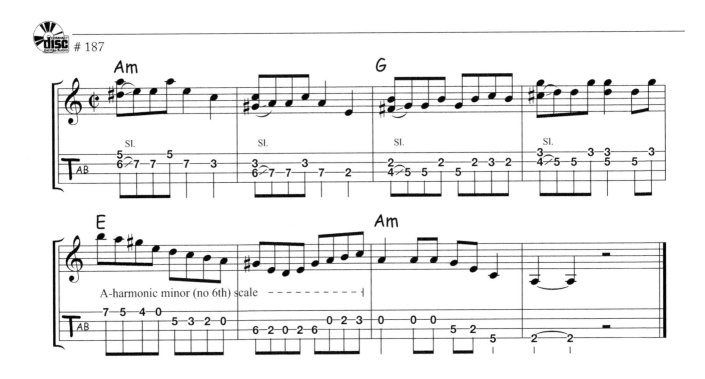

Conclusion: As seen from a harmonic point of view, the A-harmonic minor scale (or the A-harmonic (no 6th) scale) might be the right scale to use with the V chord in minor, but we shouldn't forget that, as was the case with horizontal playing, an A-minor scale was successful when used the whole way through the chord-progression, also on the E chord. In other words: Playing melodically, using the A-minor scale alone could also be a tool to use with the E chord (not only with horizontal playing, but also with vertical playing).

The fact that vertical playing is kind of difficult to handle (because of its many rules), make lot of improvisers prefer the use of horizontal playing. The well-trained improviser would also be able to skip back and forth between horizontal and vertical playing, in order to vary his improvisation the most. But for now, we don't need to worry about well-trained improvisers, just concentrate on what kind of minor key tools you like the most.

Take care of the fact that some minor key tunes modulate into a major key in the chorus, which mean that the chorus should be treated the same as a normal major-key tune (pentatonic scales instead of horizontal playing).

ASSIGNMENTS

1. Pick out a minor key tune to use for horizontal playing (all minor scales can be found in the appendix).

2. You could also try to figure out which scales to use with the minor chords (don't forget that the minor (no 6th) scale is very versatile).

3. If the tune you chose has a V chord, then consider what scale to use with it (harm. minor scale, harm. minor (no 6th) scale or the pure minor scale. Don't forget that all of these scales start on the root of the key.) See the appendix.

4. Try to use vertical playing with your tune.

5. If you like double-stops, then try to figure out some minor chord double-stops.

CHAPTER 22: The Blues Sound

Bluegrass is a style of music that has lots of influences. One of the most characteristic influences might be the blues. As we learned about the spices (see chapter 9), we learned that the use of the ♭7 would provide us with a bluesy sound. Another tool to use in order to get a bluesy sound would be the use of the blues scale. The blues scale was invented by blues musicians as a scale to use for composing songs having a sad "flavor," but also a scale to improvise on using "horizontal playing" (see the previous chapter).

The blues scale is a scale that has a "minor sound," as you can hear by playing the A-blues scale.

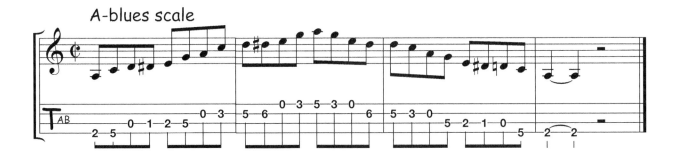

Even though the blues scale has a "minor sound," the scale is mostly used for improvising in major keys. A common blues chord progression would have twelve measures using the following structure:

The blues scheme:

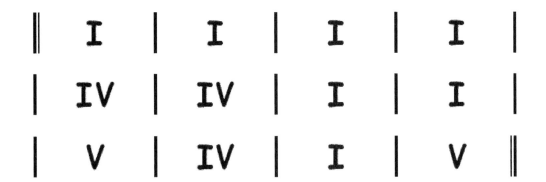

Of course the blues scheme also has lots of variations. Adding a flatted seven to the chords is also commonly used. The following example will show us how the blues scale could be used with a blues chord progression, using horizontal playing.

117

Blues solo

As you could hear, the blues scale has a very characteristic sound. It works really well with a blues song, but does it also work with a bluegrass song as well? Yes it does! The blues scale can also be used in bluegrass, but a couple of rules have to be observed.

Rule No 1:   Play melodically. Force yourself to play up and down the scale (as we did in the previous chapter, learning the use of horizontal playing).

Rule No 2:   Try to emphasize the root of the played chord. Start on it, stay on it, accent it, or play around it.

Rule No 3:   Get home on the last line, as we learned in chapter 12 ("Last Line" Licks).

Check out the use of the blues scale with a standard bluegrass chord progression.

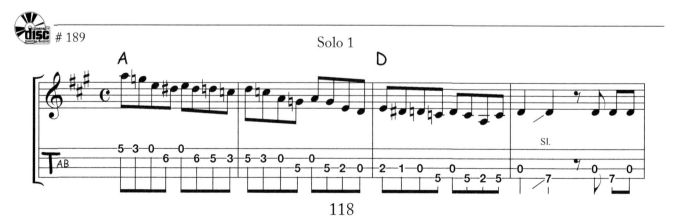

Solo 1

As you could hear, it sounded great. The blues scale can surely be used for horizontal playing with major-key tunes. But, and this is quite important: The blues scale should not be looked at as "the new main tool" to use. Use it in order to give your improvisation a bluesy sound, which would work well with bluesy bluegrass tunes. The blues scale also comes into its own right on more modern/progressive bluegrass tunes.

The blues scale could also be mixed up with other scales and tools, as done in the following example, in which the D chord (IV chord) would be treated "normally" using the major pentatonic-scale and "spices."

190   Solo 2

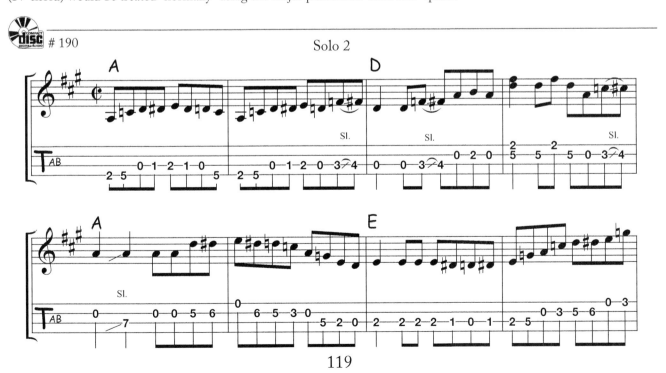

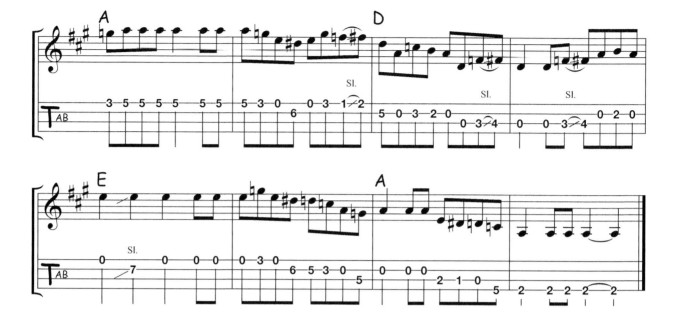

In order to emphasize the major tonality of the key, another trick to use is to include the major 3rd in the scale. This is commonly used with the one-chord (ex. the A chord in A-major). In fact, we already know the movement going from the minor 3rd to the major 3rd, and that's exactly what we'll add to the blues scale as well. The major 3rd will be marked in the tablature.

191

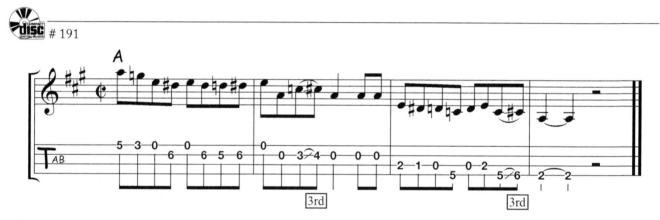

Mountain minor:

The mountain minor, which sometimes is also referred to as the modal sound, is an original old-time sound having a "minor flavor." Banjo players often retune their banjos into this minor tuning in order to achieve the right sound. The mountain minor songs were probably not accompanied in the early days, but later on as old-time and bluegrass bands wanted to put some chords with the tunes, a question arose: "Is it a minor tune or is it a major tune having a "minor flavor"? The resolution was surely influenced by the number of chords that the guitar players knew. The same song was sometimes accompanied as a minor tune and some other times as a "minor flavored" major tune. Other times the back-up was kind of simplified by playing basically only one chord (two at the most). This type of accompaniment is often referred to as modal playing/the modal sound.

The "minor flavored" major sound:

In cases where the mountain minor tunes were accompanied as a major tune, a couple of "new" major chords were often added: The ♭III chord and the ♭VII chord. To define these two "new" chords, we need to lower the third and the seventh step of the key which is played. In the key of A-major the flatted third would be the tone c and the flatted seven would be the tone g. Our two "new" chords would consequently be the chords C and G. These two major chords are actually chords belonging to the key of A-minor. But in connection with the common chords of A-major (A, D and E), the C and the

G chords would provide us with some kind of "minor flavor," which would be really necessary in order to harmonize the mountain minor tunes. Sometimes guitar players (or other musicians) leave out the third of the one-chord while accompanying, in order to avoid a definite major or minor sound. Over the years, many bluegrass tunes were composed using the mountain minor sound as a model.

The following two examples will illustrate how the exact same mountain minor melody could be harmonized both in major and in minor. The number of ways to harmonize a mountain minor tune is almost endless. The following self-composed melody is based on the "minor (no 6th) scale" (like most all mountain minor tunes).

192

Mountain Fever (major)

Composed by J. Rübner-Petersen

193

Mountain Fever (minor)

Composed by J. Rübner-Petersen

121

A perfect match:

If you have a mountain minor style of tune with which you need to improvise, the blues scale would really come to its right. The fact that the mountain minor tunes are compatible with both major and minor keys doesn't influence our use of the blues scale (the blues scale is usable with both major and minor harmonized tunes). In the following example, the sound of the blues scale used on a mountain minor tune is demonstrated. The chord progression is in major, including the two "mountain minor chords," the ♭III and the ♭VII.

Solo 3

Notice that some mountain minor style tunes also could be treated as non-bluesy, using pentatonic scale based playing when improvising. Play the following example in which the previous chord progression is used. As you can see, only pentatonic-scale based playing is used. I've tried to avoid the use of the ♭7 on the ♭III and the ♭VII chords (C and G) which wouldn't sound right in this case.

Solo 4

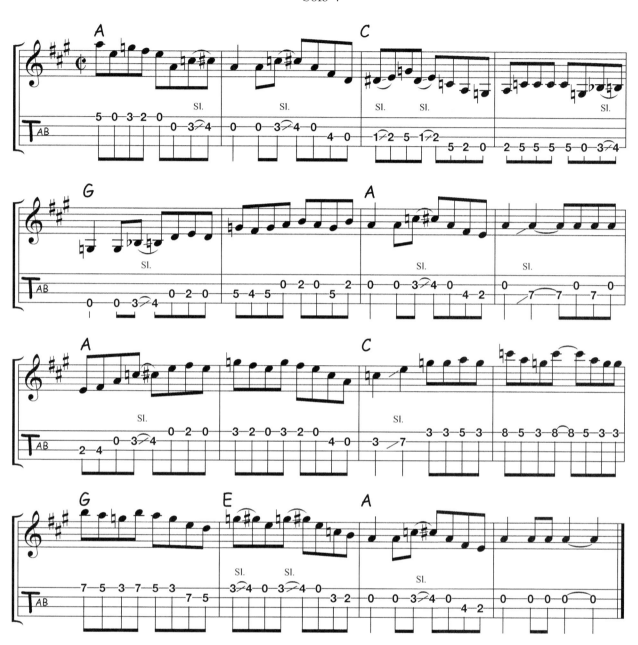

Another scale to use for improvisation on mountain minor tunes would be the minor-pentatonic scale. This scale is similar to the blues scale and will be more in-depth in Chapter 26 (Other "Spices"). See also "Pretty Polly" (Chapter 25).

The extended blues scale:

Another trick to use is the extension of the blues scale. By adding the major 2nd to the blues scale, a new scale is created (let's call it the extended blues scale). This "new" scale is kind of a mixture of the blues scale and the minor (no 6th) scale (see Chapter 20). The extended blues scale is quite often used for improvising on bluesy or modern/progressive style major tunes. But with minor tunes (and mountain minor tunes) the extended blues scale will also work out very well, in order to give the minor tune a touch of blues. Listen to the sound of the extended blues scale.

Extended blues scale

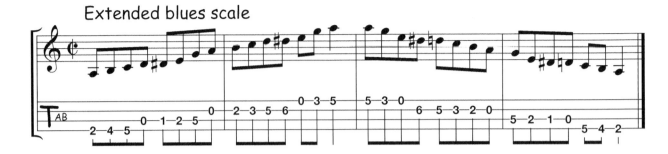

A or Am

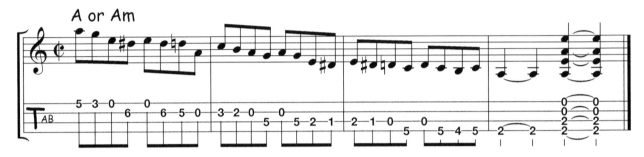

ASSIGNMENTS

1. Try to think of a couple of tunes, with which the blues scale would come to its own right. Pick out one of them and try to improvise on it.

2. Compose a mountain minor tune/chord progression in the key of A-major, using the chords: A, C, G, D, and E

3. Compose some licks using the blues scale or the extended blues scale.

CHAPTER 23: Monroe Style

The Monroe style is a style invented by Bill Monroe as a tool to use for improvising on tunes in the keys of B- and B♭-major. Monroe's high-pitched way of singing (also referred to as the high lonesome sound), made him have to choose to play many of his tunes in some uncommon keys like B- and B♭-major in order to get the sound that he was looking for. The main idea behind the Monroe style is to be able to improvise a solo in the same position as where the back-up chords are played, without using any open strings at all. The Monroe style is based on arpeggios and double-stop positions up the neck. But unlike what we have learned in previous chapters, the Monroe style basically is played in one position only.

In order to be able to understand the Monroe style, it's necessary to know the arpeggios belonging to the "bluegrass chop chords." Let's concentrate on the key of B-major which has the three main chords: B, E and F♯. Check out the following chords and their associated arpeggios.

The B chord:

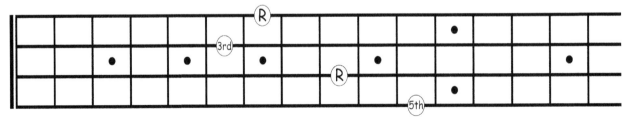

B-major arpeggio

The E chord:

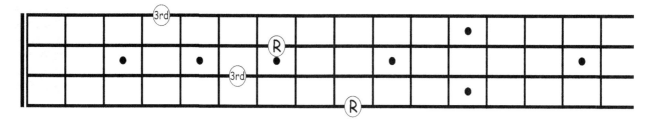

E-major arpeggio

The F♯ chord:

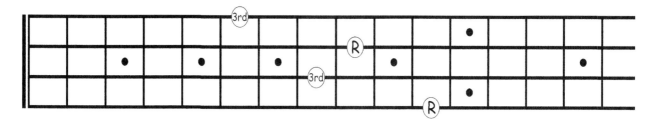

F♯ -major arpeggio

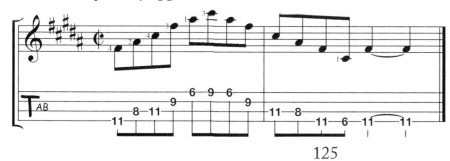

On the "E chop chord" I've added the rarely fingered/played tone g♯ (on the first string) in order to understand the arpeggios better. When "chopping" the chords, it is common to only hit the lower two or three strings. Knowing this, it's obvious that when "chopping" the F♯ chord, the tone on the first string (a♯) doesn't need to be fingered either. The "B chop chord" is always fingered as written in the box system.

How to play the Monroe style:

The best way to learn this style is to play and memorize a couple of transcribed solos. Although the Monroe style is a lick-oriented style, we don't need to know a lot of licks in order to be able to start improvising something useful. As "first aid" to those of you who have never dealt with the Monroe style, I've written out some solos to play using common licks and movements. Don't forget to compare the licks to their related "chop chords" and arpeggios. Do you see the connection?

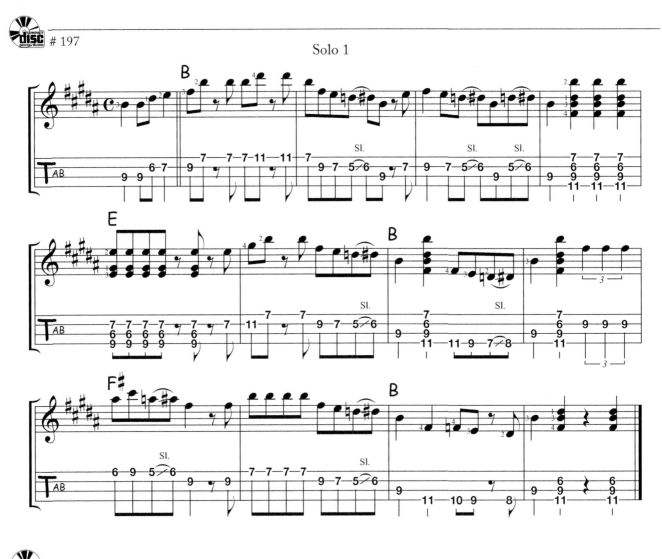

197

Solo 1

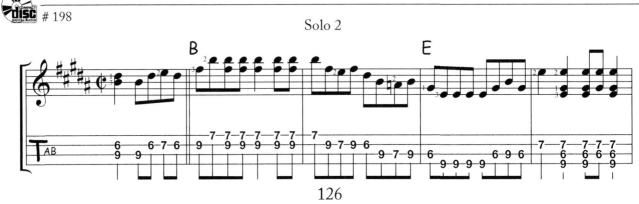

198

Solo 2

126

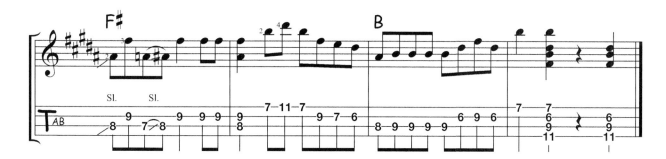

 # 199

Solo 3

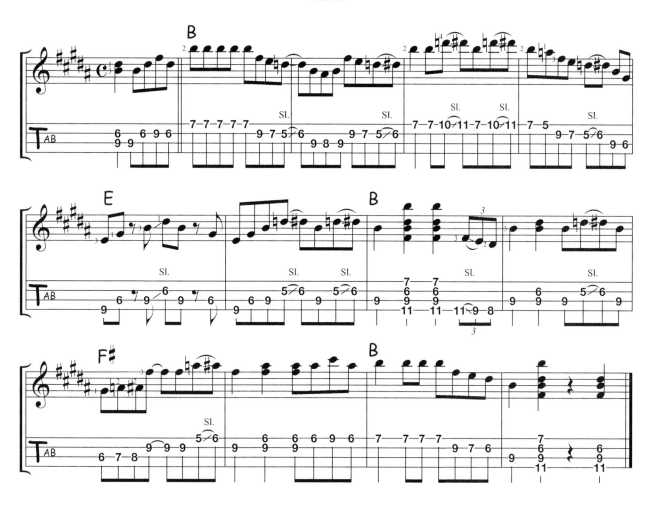

 # 200

Solo 4

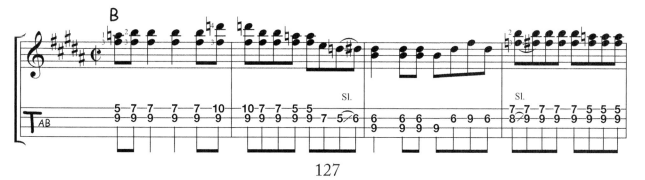

127

Analyzing the Solos:

As you might have noticed, the Monroe style is a tonic-oriented style. The tonic is just another name for the "one-chord" of the key in which the song is played. The tonic (the I chord) is often observed in advance by playing tonic-oriented licks in the last bar before appearing on the I chord. This technique of "anticipating the tonic," only works if the lick leads back to the root-tone of the tonic. By playing tonic-oriented licks on the IV chord (the E chord in B-major) some non-harmonic tones will be produced, because of the d♯ tone. But the leading effect is there and it works!

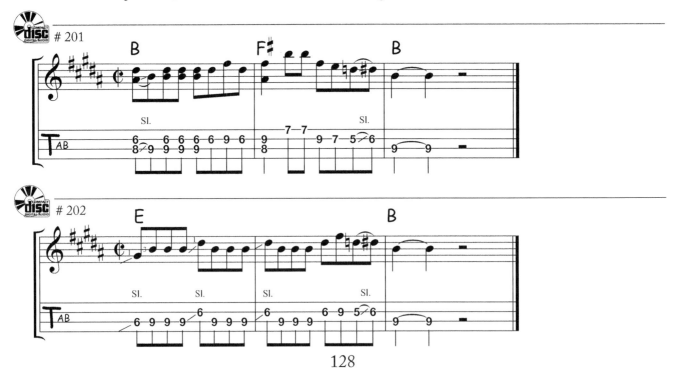

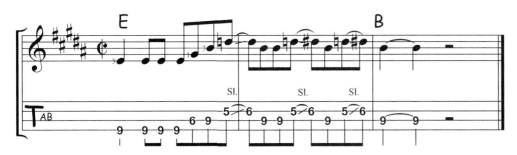

By playing through the four solos, it's obvious to see that Solo 4 is more bluesy than the other three solos. This blues feeling comes from the use of the ♭3 and the ♭7 with the tonic (I chord) and the ♭7 with the IV chord. The use of the ♭3 (on the first string) is commonly used when improvising in the Monroe style on a bluesy bluegrass tune. Check out how the first two measures of Solo 1 could get a bluesy touch by changing the major 3rd to a minor 3rd.

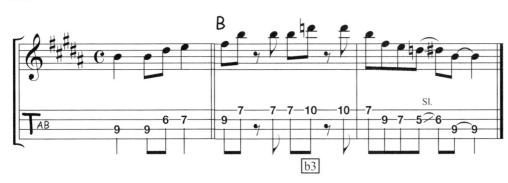

The ♭7 as leading tone:

Another common technique to use is the "♭7 leading effect." Beyond giving the music a bluesy feel, the ♭7 could also be looked at as a leading tone which leads us into the next chord. This leading effect only works if the following chord contains a chord tone half a step below the played ♭7. Common movements in which the ♭7 could be used as a leading tone are: I chord → IV chord or V chord → I chord. In order to get the right effect, the ♭7 has to be played just before changing chords. A common trick is the chromatic movement from Root to ♭7 as you'll see in the following examples. Chromatics will also be covered in Chapter 26 (Other Spices).

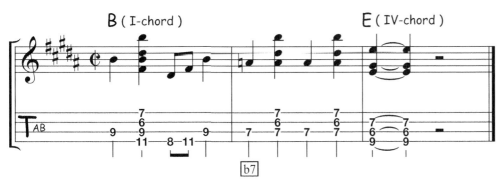

206

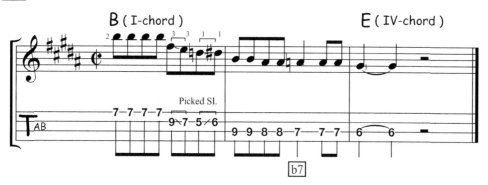

207

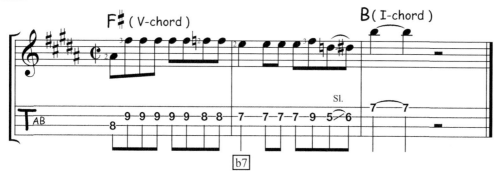

Mixing the licks:

As already mentioned, we only need a "handful" of licks in order to be able to play in the Monroe style. Don't be afraid of playing your Monroe style licks more then once while improvising (repetition is commonly used in Monroe style). In the following solo, I've tried to mix up the already learned Monroe style licks with a new chord progression. To assist you, I've indicated which solos I got my licks from and where the technique of "anticipating the tonic" is used.

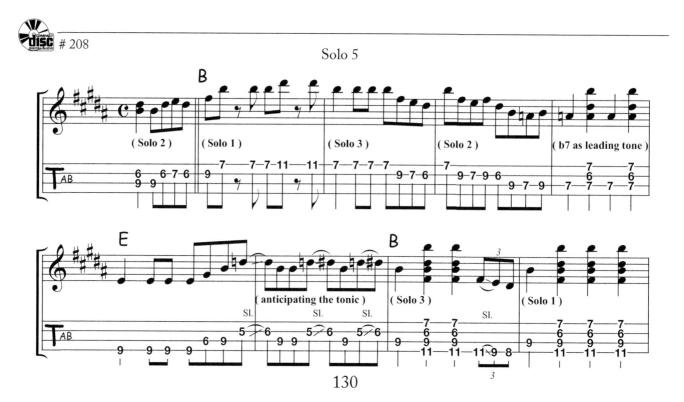

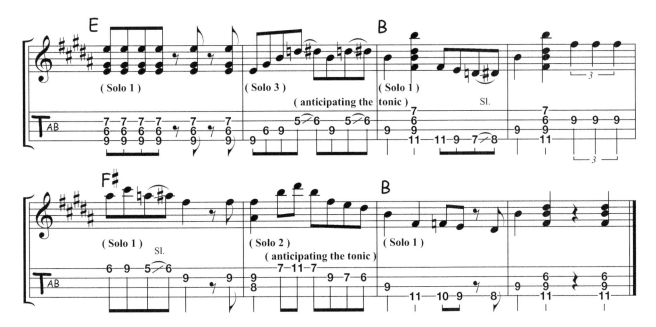

Down strokes:

Notice that a common technique in medium and slow tunes is the use of down-stroke picking. Down-stroke picking works very well on Monroe style licks and can be used the whole way through your improvising. Changing between alternate (down/up) picking and down-stroke picking can also work out quite impressively.

ASSIGNMENTS

1. Play one of the solos from the chapter, using down strokes only.

2. Try to compose a Monroe style solo to a tune in the key of B-major.

3. Transpose a well learned Monroe style solo down to B♭ by moving every tone one fret below.

4. Transpose the same solo to some other keys.

5. Learn or transcribe some other Monroe style solos in order the get some more ideas to use by improvising.

CHAPTER 24: Cross Picking

Cross picking is primary a technique used by guitar players in order to provide the rolling sound of the "three-finger style" bluegrass banjo. The cross picking technique is (as the name indicates) basically a technique where several strings are picked one after the other in some kind of symmetrical order. On the mandolin, the use of cross picking could be divided into two categories: two- and three-string cross picking. "Three-string cross picking" is basically the same as what we know from the guitar, in contrast to the "two-string cross picking" which is a more "simplified" mandolin technique. Even though the "three-string cross picking style" might be the basic one, I've chosen to start out with the "two-string cross picking technique" because of the fact that this technique is more usable for improvising.

The two-string cross picking technique:

The "two-string cross picking technique" is based on a "three-note sequence" which is repeated for one or more measures. In the following example the "three-note sequence" is repeated two times followed by two extra notes. This grouping could be referred as the 3 - 3 - 2 permutation. With the "two-string cross picking technique" alternate picking is used (see the Introduction in the beginning of the book).

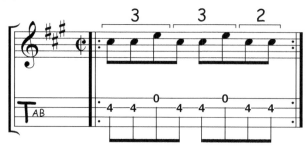

As you can see, only two different notes were used (the c♯ and the e). These two notes both belong to the A chord. The 3 - 3 - 2 permutation can naturally also be used on other chords as demonstrated in the next example.

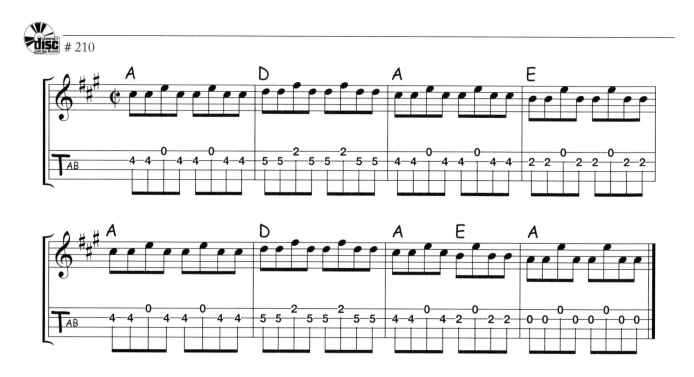

The following two groupings: the 2 - 3 - 3 permutation and the 1 - 3 - 3 - 1 permutation could also be used when improvising. Notice that the 1 - 3 - 3 - 1 permutation starts on the first string, which might be useful in some situations.

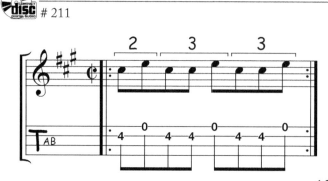

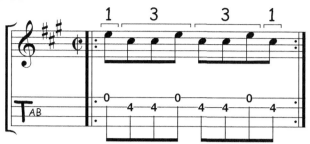

Before proceeding with this chapter, try to use the two new groupings with the same chord progression that we used with the 3 - 3 - 2 permutation.

Slides:

On the 3 - 3 - 2 permutation, a slide could be quite useful as shown in the following example. As you can see, the first note is slid into the second note from a half-step below. A hammer-on could also be used as a substitute to the slide.

213

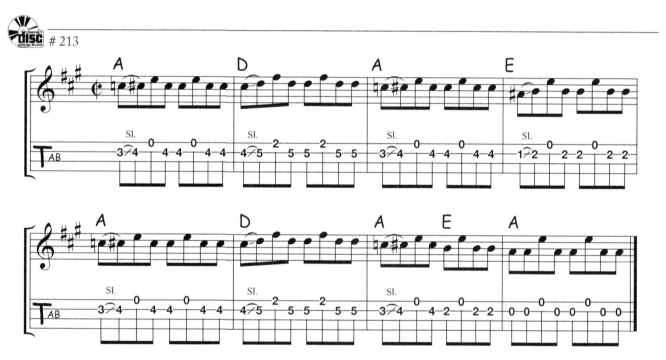

Other groupings:

Check out the following "two measure" groupings, in which the "three-note sequences" really make the lines come out with an interesting sound.

214

215

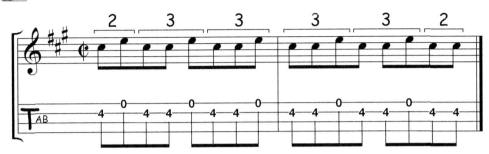

216

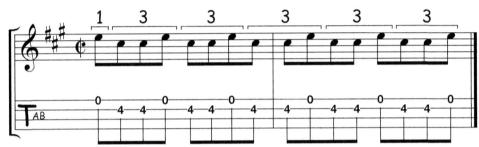

Melodic lines:

If you want to extend the cross picking sound, the use of a melodic line on top of the "three-note sequences" would work out very well. In order to demonstrate this, I've written out two examples to play. The first example is kind of straight bluegrass compared to the second one, which is done in a country rag style.

217

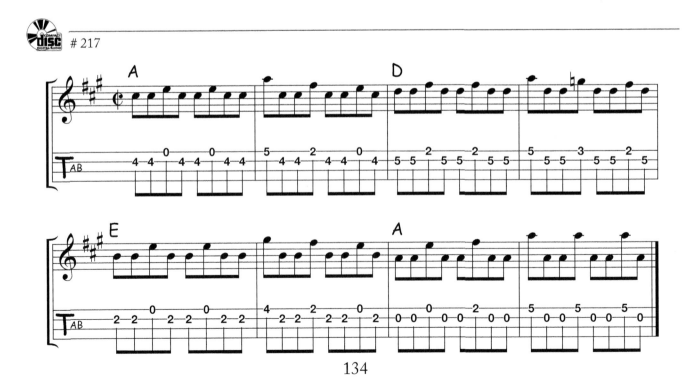

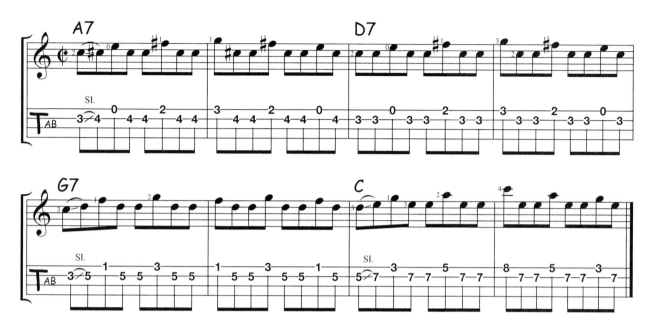

Mixing the ideas:

When improvising using cross picking, you don't have to stick to cross picking alone. Mixing pentatonic licks with cross picking lines can give your improvisation some interesting combinations. Play the following two examples in order to get the feeling of how cross picking can be used. The second example will show us how to handle a non-key related chord using cross picking.

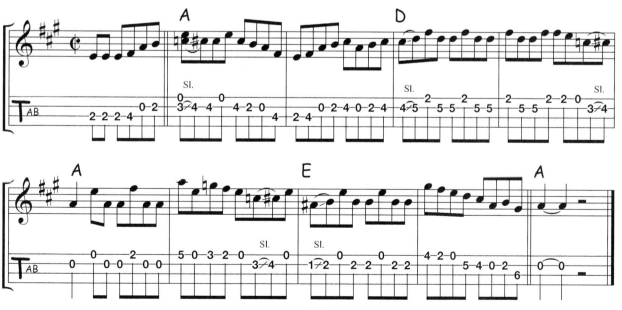

220

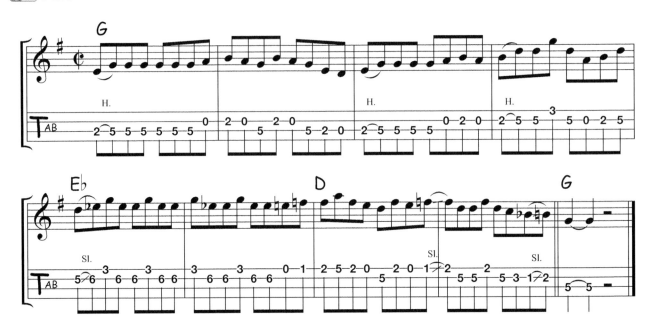

The three-string cross picking technique:

"Three-string cross picking" is also based on chord tones. But in contrast to two-string cross picking where alternate picking is used, the "three-string cross picking" technique implements other picking patterns. The following examples will demonstrate the system. Be aware of the stroke directions.

 # 221

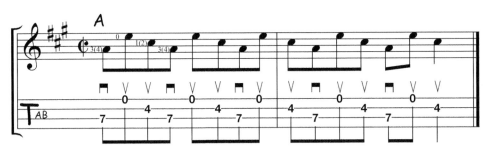

 # 222

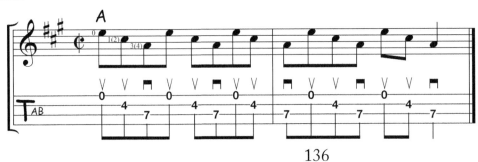

136

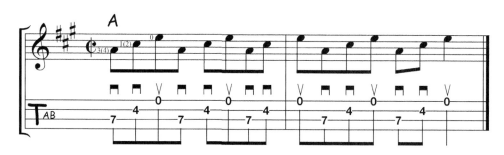

"Three-string cross picking" has an even more open sound than "two-string cross picking" and is basically nearly always played on the three high strings. The use of the open E string has also become commonly used with "three-string cross picking," especially on chords containing an e tone. But the open E string could also be used on chords not containing an e tone, as long as the e tone belongs to the key of the tune being played. To demonstrate this, take a look at the D chord in the next example played in the key of A-major. The second example shows us the same chord progression in G-major using different cross picking patterns.

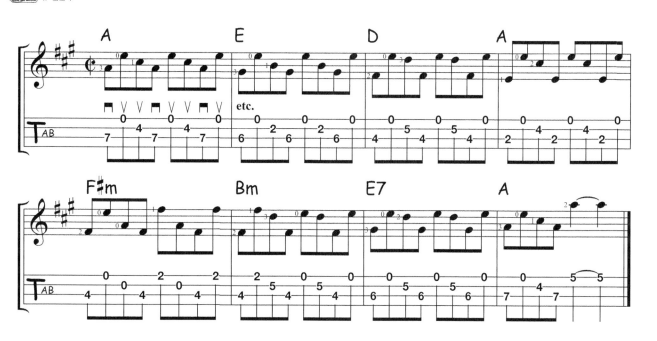

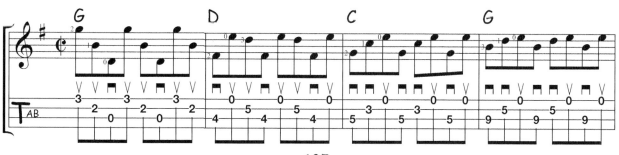

137

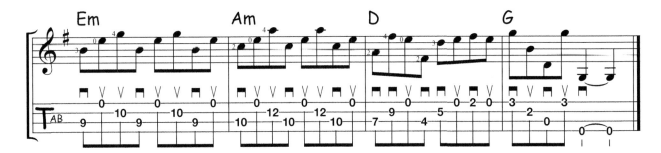

"Three-string cross picking" can of course also be mixed with pentatonic licks and other ideas, but to me "three-string cross picking" sounds best if it's used on more than one bar containing chord changes. To be able to improvise using "three-string cross picking" a thorough knowledge about chords and their chord tones is needed. Don't forget that lots of the things we have learned about double-stops (chord-tones), can be used for figuring out cross picking chord positions.

Other ideas:

The cross picking patterns that we have learned in this chapter are all basics. The amounts of ways to vary these patterns is nearly endless. Also the picking directions of the strokes could be played differently in order to get another sound. For example, some mandolin players use alternate picking on "three-string cross picking." Don't hesitate to try out new ideas and variations.

ASSIGNMENTS

1. Try to figure out some double-stops to use for "two-string cross picking" on a well-known song. Pick out one of the cross-picking permutations and use it the whole way through. You might have to write your ideas down in order to not lose track of the patterns.

2. Choose an easy chord progression to use for mixing up already learned licks and the "two-string cross picking."

3. Write out a solo for a medium speed/slow song utilizing "three-string cross picking" patterns.

CHAPTER 25: The Melody

Up to this point, the improvisation tools that we have learned were all based on the chords/keys of the tunes played. But what about the melody? Shouldn't the melody be the guideline for every played solo? Actually, the answer would be no. A solo can be based on the melody, but it doesn't have to be. Over the years, while learning about bluegrass improvisation, I discovered that a lot of solos weren't based on the melody, without realizing it at first. The main reason for this was probably the fact that I kept on having the lead vocal melody in my mind, as the soloist was playing his solo. The solo just came out as a perfect "accompaniment" to the melody which I still was hearing inside my head. This kind of illusion only works if the solos are based on the harmonic structure of the tune, but the spirit of the tune is also important here. The spirit of a tune could also be described as the character of the tune. Is it a modal tune, does it have a strong or a slightly bluesy thought, is the tune traditional or modern, or even jazzy? All these characteristics are just as important as the melody itself, and should surely be kept in mind while choosing ideas for your improvisation.

The Melody:

To be able to improvise using the melody as a guideline is actually not so easy. At first we need to know the melody by heart and then we have to be able to play around it. Some musicians are really good in picking up melodies on the spot, which implies a good ear for melodic lines and their structures (skills which can be trained). If you aren't that good in picking up melodies, you have to stick to improvisations based on the harmonic structure of the tune, or to arrange some melody-based solos. To indicate the melody in the beginning of a solo before going into chord-based improvisation is also a commonly-used technique. A split melody/improvised solo will also give the listener the same kind of "hearing the melody" illusion which I talked about before. If you are playing in a band where you don't have to play improvised solos, it's certainly a good idea to work out some solos based on the melody. Especially if you have to do the opening break on a tune– melody-based solo shouldn't be missing.

The structure of a bluegrass tune:

In order to be able to compose a melody based solo, it's important to know the structure of the chosen tune. Fortunately, most standard bluegrass tunes are based on the same 4 x 4 measure structure:

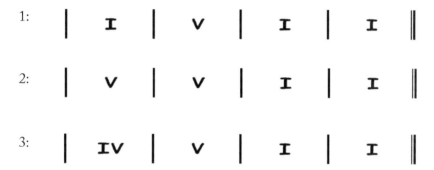

Before starting to figure out how the melody goes, we need to know the precise order of the chords. As a help to you, it's good to know that most standard bluegrass tunes have one of the following three "last lines."

1:   | I | V | I | I ‖

2:   | V | V | I | I ‖

3:   | IV | V | I | I ‖

Alternative "last lines" can be seen in tunes with short verses (four / eight measures). Notice, for example, that blues tunes have a 3 x 4 measure structure. Some tunes also have lines containing an extra measure or even a half measure. But for now let's concentrate on the straight ones.

Will The Circle Be Unbroken:

A tune that all bluegrass musicians know is "Will the Circle Be Unbroken." It's a perfect tune to use for demonstrating the standard 4 x 4 measure structure and the "last line." Take a look at the chord progression and its structure.

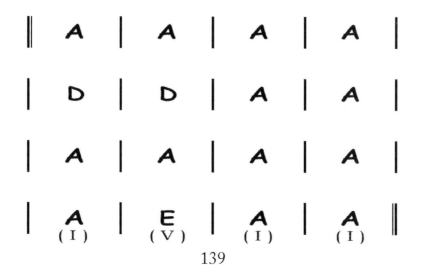

As you can see, this tune has the I - V - I - I "last line" at the end. The I - V - I - I "last line" is also the most common "last line" in bluegrass music and might be found in nearly every other standard bluegrass tune. Use this knowledge about the "last lines" in order to check out if the chord progression to a song is written out correctly. A big problem which I've seen with many of my students is the lack of skills in figuring out the precise placement of the melody in the measures of the tune. As a good way to determine the placement of the melody, we'll use the technique of writing out the song lyrics on the chord progression chart. You might have to sing the song while playing the chords in order to figure out where to write in the lyrics. Use the spots where the chords change as a guideline to where we are in the tune. ATTENTION!!! Beware of the fact that in most cases the melody starts before the first beat of the tune. Also, "Will the Circle Be Unbroken" starts on an upbeat, as you can see in the following chart.

Will the Circle Be Unbroken
(Trad.)

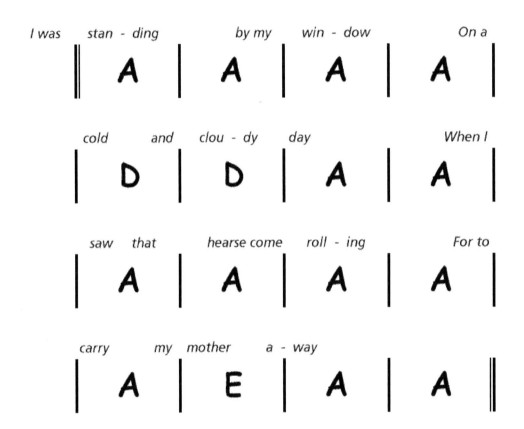

As I wrote in the words of the lyrics, I also attempted to write them at their correct locations within the measures. Having a lyric/chord chart done is absolutely the best preparation before writing down the melody of a tune.

The melody to a song is, as we all know, made out of a note line as sung/played within a certain rhythm. A correct answer to how a melody should go doesn't exist. Each vocalist sings a certain song their own way, depending on how they learned it, or how they want it to sound. The melody line which we need for our melody-based solos should be kept as simple as possible. If we have a simple melody, it's easier to make up some interesting variations for it. In the following example I've written out the melody to "Will the Circle Be Unbroken." Also the rhythm of the melody is kept as simple as possible in order to keep the melody at its most basic level.

Will the Circle Be Unbroken (Trad.)

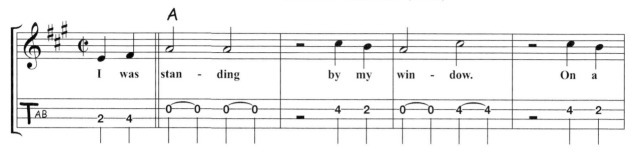

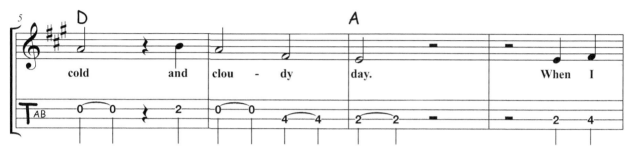

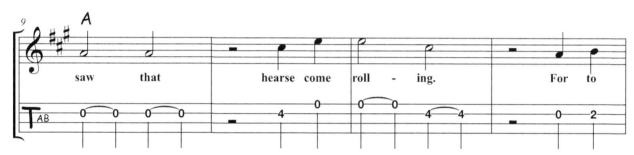

The next thing that I've done is to write out a melody-based solo. This solo is kept simple with only some small variations in the melody, mixed with a couple of easy fill-in runs. The techniques and ideas that I've used to arrange this solo are similar to the "easy playing" that we learned about in Chapter 8. The notes in the parentheses shouldn't be accented as much as the other ones.

Will the Circle (solo 1)

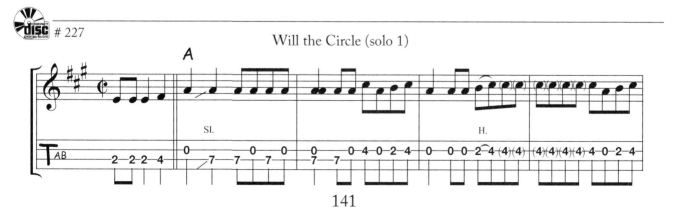

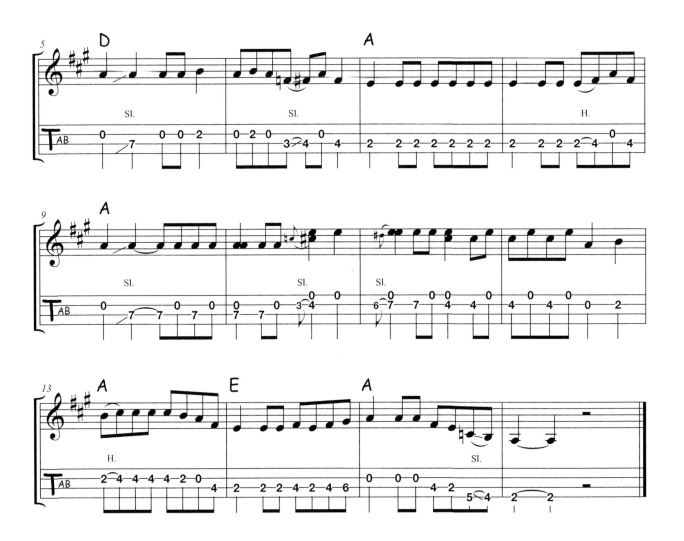

To arrange a melody-based solo is a puzzle which might take a couple of tries before it come out perfectly. The number of ways to arrange a melody-based solo is endless, which means that your solution depends completely on how you would like it to sound– your taste. In my second arrangement to "Will the Circle Be Unbroken," I've tried to put in a lot of runs and licks in order to give you an idea on how varied a melody based solo could be. But as you'll see, it's still based on the melody.

 # 228

Will the Circle (solo 2)

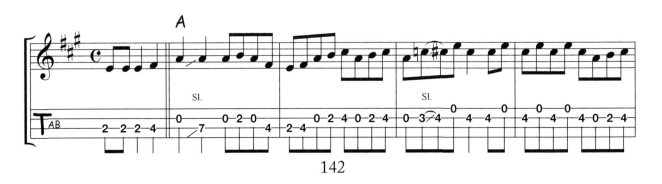

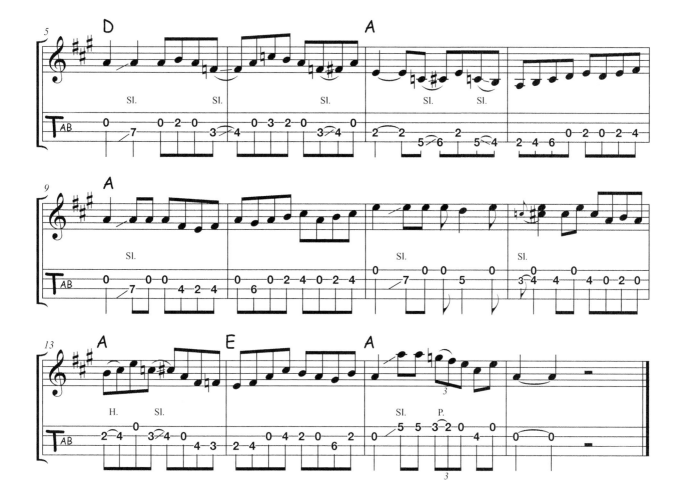

White House Blues:

I've picked out the song "White House Blues" because of the melody, which isn't as root oriented as many other songs. Root oriented! What does that mean? Actually it's quite simple: If the melody is based on, or implicates the roots of the chords a lot, the song could be described as being root oriented. For example, the melody to "Will the Circle Be Unbroken" is kind of circled around the a-tone, which is the root of the A chord. I won't describe "Will the Circle Be Unbroken" as being a strong root-oriented song, but compared with the "White House Blues" it is. Whether a song is root oriented or not, doesn't affect the quality of the tune. If we take a look at the melody of "White House Blues," you'll see that it doesn't implicate the root of the chords until nearly the end of the verse. The melody has a slight blues feel and the form of the song is based on the 3 x 4 measure blues tune structure.

229

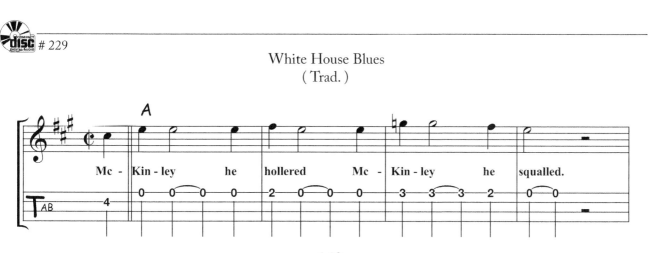

White House Blues
(Trad.)

143

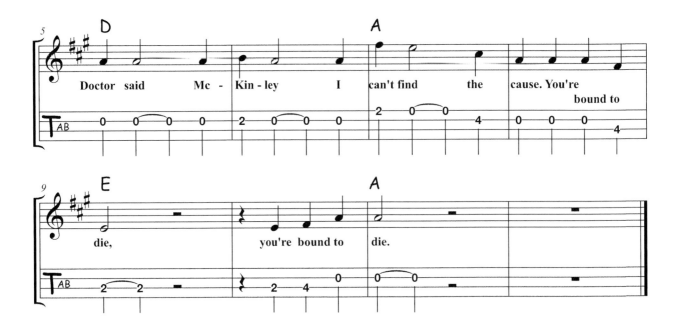

As we learned about the pentatonic licks back in Chapter 4, we had some different licks starting on the root, the 3rd and the 5th of the played chord. But as we kept on learning about improvisation, you might have noticed that the licks starting on the root were used more often than the other ones. The "root licks" are actually easier to use because of the fact that they "go along" with the chord changes. If you improvise using mostly "root licks," the listener will also hear the chord changes in your playing. To mix up melody-oriented playing with some chord-based licks is another way to create an interesting solo. Take a look at my solo "White House Blues" and notice the use of a "root lick" on the D chord. On the last bar of the A chord before changing to the D chord, I also skipped the melody in order to play root oriented. The mix of melody and licks in a solo is a good way to bring out some individuality to the tune.

 # 230

White House Blues (solo)

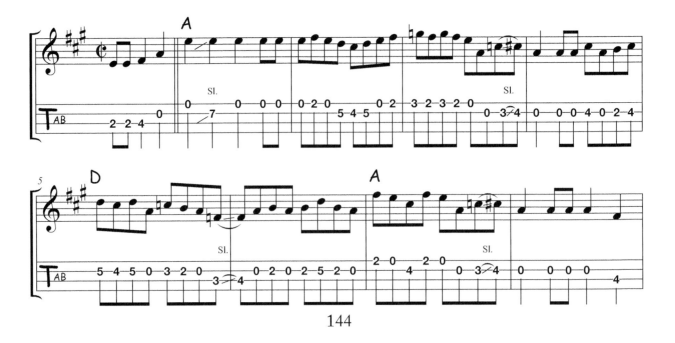

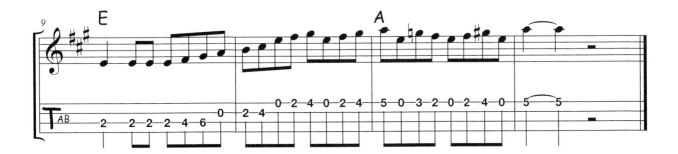

John Hardy:

The song "John Hardy" is also a standard bluegrass tune which I'd like to demonstrate another way of mixing melody-oriented playing and licks. But before doing this, let's take a look at the straight melody line (kept simple).

231

John Hardy
(Trad.)

145

My idea for the "John Hardy" solo was to stay true to the melody all the way until the D chord and then change to lick-oriented playing. This way of changing somewhere in the middle of a solo will certainly surprise the listener. The lick-oriented part could surely also be improvised and in that way kept open to new ideas. I added some cross picking to the melody part of "John Hardy" as an example of how it would be done. On the D chord I just let the fingers do the work, playing licks and tricks.

232

John Hardy (solo)

146

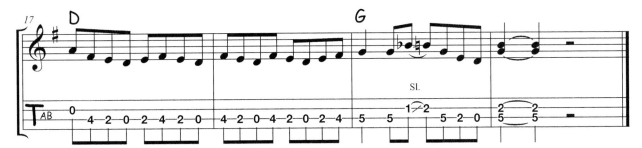

Dark Hollow:

In "Dark Hollow" I'm nearly back to straight lick-oriented playing. I start out the solo by touching the melody for the first three measures and then I leave it behind, using licks only. I think this solo might give you the "illusion of hearing the melody" without having it directly played. You might have to sing a couple of verses before playing the solo, in order to get the right illusion. But at first play the straight melody and then turn to the "magical solo" (please let it work !!!).

233

Dark Hollow (Trad.)

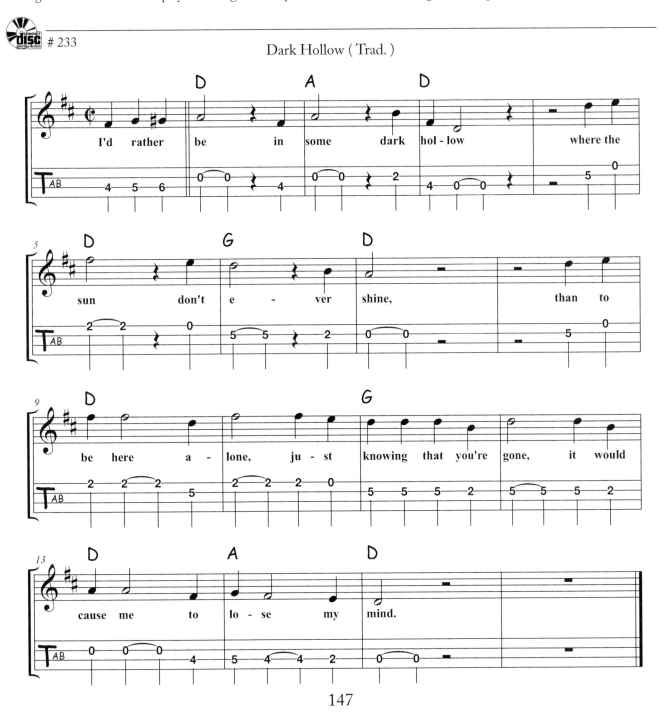

147

234

Dark Hollow (solo)

Wayfaring Stranger:

As a slow bluegrass ballad, I've chosen "Wayfaring Stranger" for my arrangement. It's in the key of A-minor and perfect to use for some double-stop playing. When we learned about double-stops (Chapter 17), we worked on major keys only. But we can surely also use the chord-tones from the minor key chords in order to harmonize some of the melody tones. The most common way to harmonize a melody tone is to add another chord tone, which is played above the original one. But the harmony tone could also be added below the melody. We don't have to harmonize every single tone of the melody, but the long-lasting ones are just perfect to harmonize using double-stops. So, actually it's quite simple: We just play the melody of the tune and every time a long-lasting tone appears, we harmonize it using a double-stop. On a slow tune as "Wayfaring Stranger," it sounds really good to use tremolos on the double-stops. But cross picking also goes very well

148

together with double-stops. In my arrangement of "Wayfaring Stranger," I didn't stick to the straight melody, but varied it in order to show you some variation ideas. A couple of times I also utilized the "harmonizing the scale" technique (see Chapter 19).

235

Wayfaring Stranger
(Trad.)

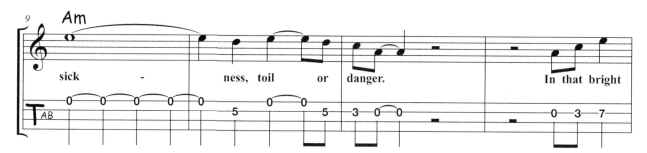

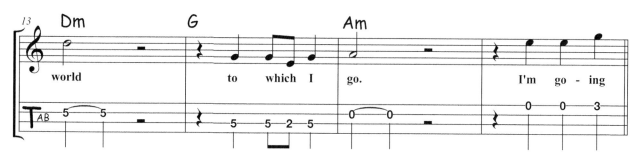

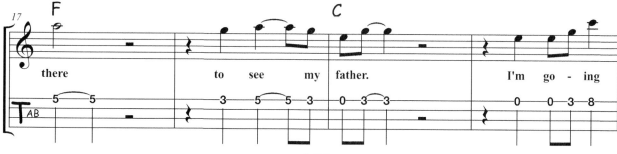

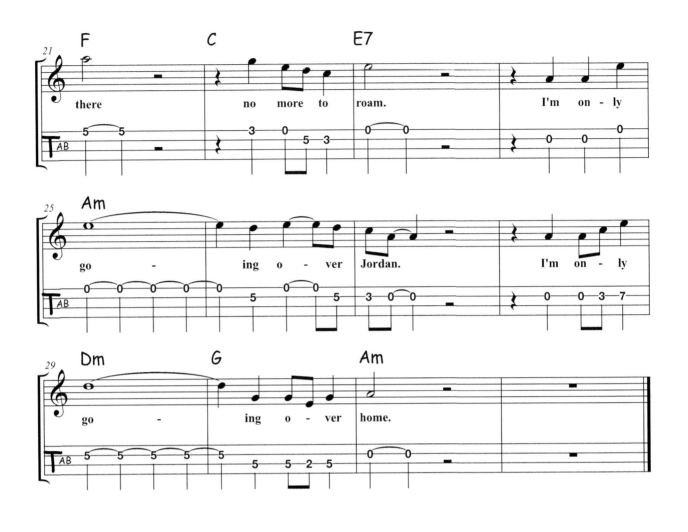

Wayfaring Stranger (solo)

Pretty Polly:

Our last tune in this chapter is the mountain minor/modal tune "Pretty Polly." As we learned about the mountain minor tunes (Chapter 22), I told you that the most common melody scale would be the minor (no 6th) scale. If we leave out the 2nd of this scale, we have a minor (no 6th and no 2nd). This scale is also called the **minor pentatonic scale**. The minor pentatonic scale will be covered in depth in the upcoming chapter. The reason I tell you about the minor pentatonic scale now is because the melody to "Pretty Polly" is based on this scale. So, let's play the B-minor pentatonic scale and the melody to "Pretty Polly."

237

Pretty Polly
(Trad.)

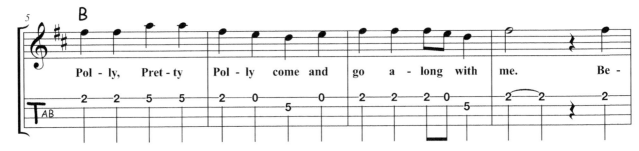

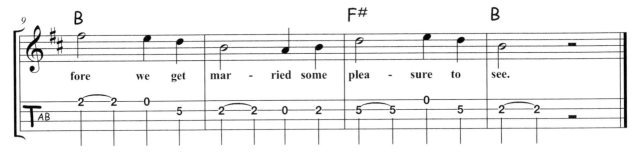

For "Pretty Polly," I've worked out two solos to play. The first one is based on the melody and uses the B-minor pentatonic scale too. The second solo is based on the B blues scale and has a more modern touch. The second solo does not really stick to the melody, but on some parts it kind of moves along with the melody as you'll hear when playing it. In fact, this kind of improvising where the solo follows the melody direction without playing the straight melody is often used by improvisers. A well-trained improviser can do this kind of "following the melody direction" easily. If you hear the melody "inside your head" while improvising and if you have a bunch of licks, tricks and ideas to use, it isn't any problem to play up and down along with the melody movements. Improvise using the technique of "following the melody direction" isn't for beginners, but it's a good thing to know about and for sure it's also a system that can be use for composing solos. So, let's have some fun playing the solos.

238

Pretty Polly (solo 1)

239

Pretty Polly (solo 2)

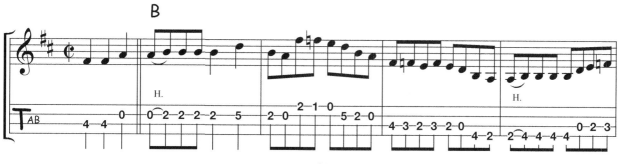

153

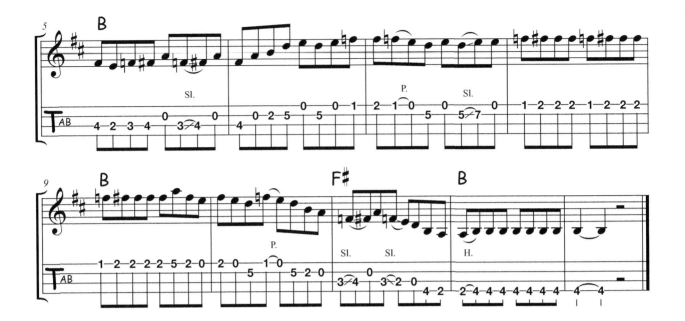

ASSIGNMENTS

1. Try to write down the chord structure chart to one of your favorite songs.

2. Write in the lyrics on the chart.

3. Figure out the basic melody line and write it down on a piece of standard notation/tablature paper. The rhythm of the melody isn't that important, but be sure that the melody is written down in the correct measures.

4. Compose a melody-based solo on the song.

CHAPTER 26: Other Spices

At this point we're slowly coming toward the end of this book. We have learned about the pentatonic scales and their "spices." We have explored our fretboard by playing double-stops up the neck. We also dug into minor keys, the blues, cross picking and the style of Bill Monroe and we have learned about different ways to play around the melody of a tune. Actually, we know a lot about improvising now and if you worked on the assignments I'm sure you've become a better improviser.

In this last chapter I've put together some of the last theoretical techniques to use for bluegrass improvising. Please consider these new "spices" as an extra thing to work on for the more advanced learners. If you haven't made it so far as to be able improvise in a jam session or in your band using pentatonic licks and tricks, I won't recommend that you to go to the last "spices" now. It might just get too confusing.

The Major scale:

It might be a riddle to you why I've chosen to wait until now to start talking about the use of the major scale as a main tool for improvisation. Of course I know that the major scale is the main scale for any major key tune (I've also learned it that way from my music teacher in school). But does it stay that way when we're talking bluegrass tunes? Yes and no–actually most bluegrass tunes do not use the whole major scale. Many bluegrass melodies are based on the pentatonic scale as you can see if you take a look at the major tunes from the last chapter. A bluesy bluegrass tune also mostly applies the flatted seventh which doesn't belong to the major scale.

It isn't that easy to improvise horizontally on a bluegrass tune using the major scale only. The major scale does not contain the "bluegrass characteristics" as the ♭3 - 3rd movement or the ♭7, which to me just makes the sound of bluegrass. But it is actually possible to use the major scale for improvising. In order to do this, it's important to play around the chord tones using the other tones from the major scale as passing tones. Doing this, we're kind of mixing up vertical and horizontal playing as you'll see in the following example in the key of C-major.

 # 240

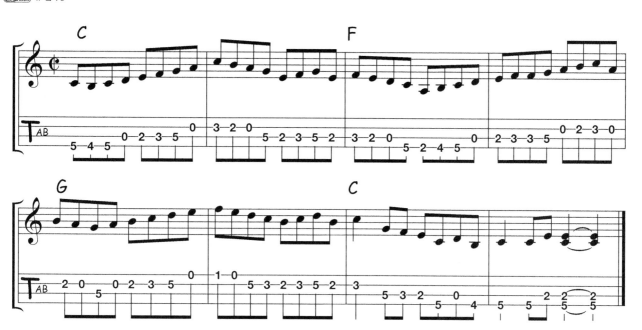

Another common major-scale trick is the use of the symmetrical sequences as we also used when we learned about the minor scale (Chapter 21). Exaggerated use of symmetrical sequences on the major scale doesn't sound that bluegrassy to me, but mixing it up with other ideas can be quite useful. In the next example I'll show you how it could be done (actually a little bit too exaggerated, but what the heck).

 # 241

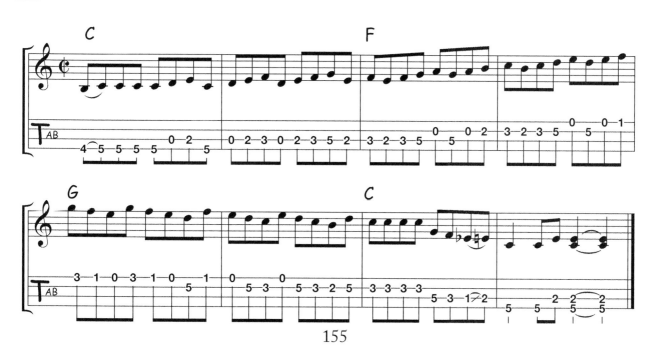

155

Key related playing:

As we learned about the pentatonic scales and their "spices," we didn't have to worry about in which key we were playing. For example could we play the same pentatonic lick on a D chord no matter if the chord was appearing in a tune in the key of D-, G-, or A-major? This way of playing around the chords is certainly the easiest access to bluegrass improvisation and it's used quite often by improvisers too. But on the other hand, it's also common to implicate the major scale of the played key. To implicate the major scale doesn't mean playing horizontally, but more to emphasize the characteristics of the major scale– the major sound. But what is the major sound, and where is the difference? O.K., I'll show you an example. In the following chord progression (in the key of C-major) every chord is treated equally. The playing is chord oriented, using pentatonic scales and the "spice" P4. The lick that is played with the C chord is transposed to the F and the G chord.

242

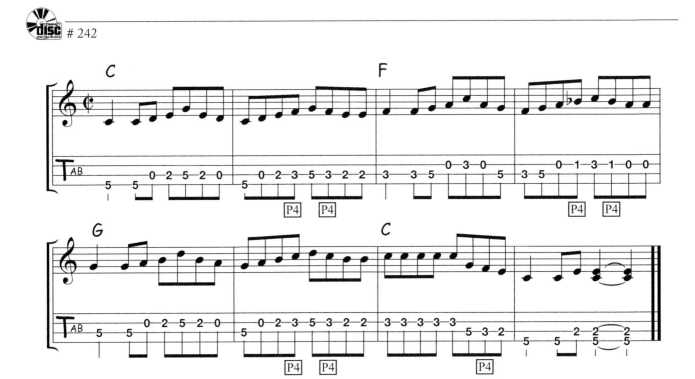

If we compare the tone material in the above example to the plain C-major scale, we'll have a small inconsistency with the F chord (the IV chord). The perfect fourth to the F chord is the tone b♭, which doesn't belong to the C-major scale. So, in order to emphasize the major sound, we need to raise the b♭ a half tone to b, while playing with the F chord (the IV chord). Listen to the change of the sound. The raised fourth is marked with the sign: #4.

243

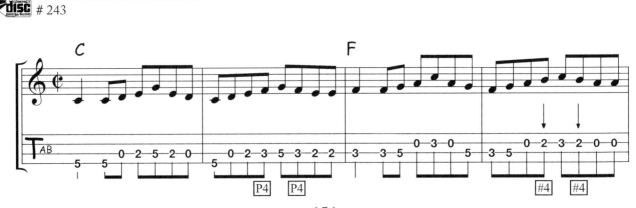

156

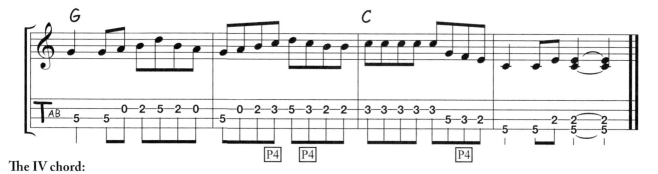

The IV chord:

As just learned, the IV chord is a chord with which we have the possibility to emphasize the sound of the played key. The big question is now: When should we use P4 as opposed to #4 with the IV chord? It's really up to you to decide which you prefer, but on bluesy bluegrass tunes, the P4 sounds the best to me. In the following solo I've tried to mix up a lot of different ideas, but I've kept strictly to the use of #4 with the IV chord. The solo is in the key of A-major, which means that the D chord is the IV chord.

244   Solo 1

The M7 and the major scale sound:

As I taught you the M7 "spice" (in Chapter 9), we learned that the M7 had to be followed up by the root of the played chord (M7 → Root). As a small reminder, I've written out an example to play in the key of C-major using pentatonic scales and the M7 "spice."

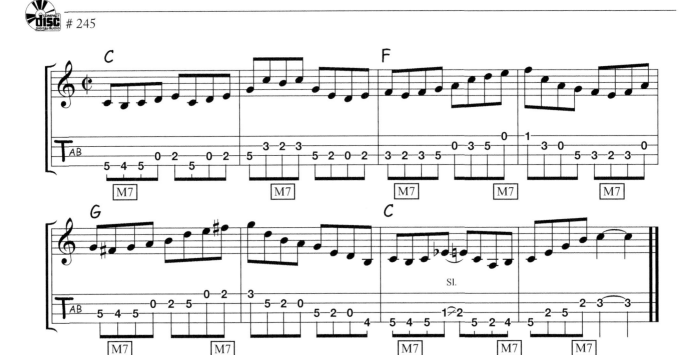

When we compare the tones of the just-played example to the plain C-major scale, we can see that one tone is different (the tone f♯ with the V chord, the G chord). The M7 → Root movement sounds really good with the V chord, but if we want to emphasize the major scale sound using other movements, we need to change the f♯ to an f. This new tone is actually the ♭7 of the G chord (V chord).

The Root → M7 → 6th movement:

A common way to emphasize the major scale sound is by using the Root → M7 → 6th movement. This movement only works out well with the I and the IV chord. With the V chord, a Root → ♭7 → 6th movement would be necessary in order to keep the major scale sound. Listen to the following example in which our new movements are demonstrated. Our first example in this chapter had a couple of Root → M7 → 6th movements too.

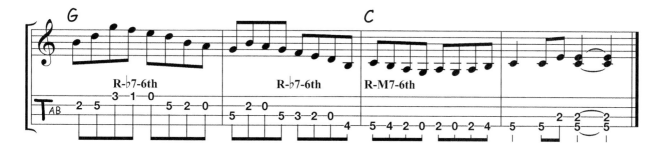

Earlier in this book we actually once played the Root → M7 → 6th movement as we learned about the F chord (Chapter 15). Try to figure out where.

NOTICE: The M7 tone should only be used as a passing tone, as long as we are concerned with bluegrass (If you want to get jazzy you might stay on it if you like). And don't forget that the plain major scale doesn't work out that well on a bluesy bluegrass tune (no ♭7 = no blues).

The mixolydian scale:

If we play a C-major scale starting on the fifth tone, our "new" scale is called G mixolydian. If we compare the G mixolydian to a G-major scale, we'll recognize that only the seventh makes the difference. The G mixolydian has a flatted seventh (♭7) and the G-major scale a major seventh (M7). The mixolydian scale is a scale to use if we want to emphasize the ♭7 sound.

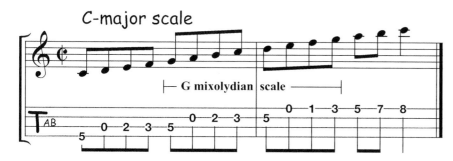

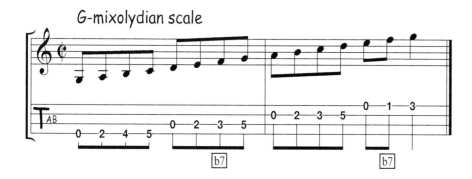

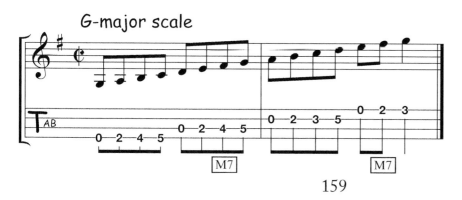

The mixolydian scale can't be used horizontally, but has to change along with the chords: G chord = G mixolydian, C chord = C mixolydian, etc. To me, a mixolydian scale is just a major pentatonic scale to which a P4 and a ♭7 are added, nothing special. So actually you might already have played the mixolydian scale without knowing it.

Other scales:

In order to make this book as clear as possible, I decided not to mention all kinds of scales. The scales I've used are all scales which could be used in bluegrass music. Other scales like Lydian and Locrian are not mentioned. If you like to know more about scales, I recommend that you read something about the theory behind the modes. Especially if you're into swing and jazz– you shouldn't miss it.

Neighbor tones:

Actually neighbor tones aren't something new to us. A neighbor tone is the tone half a step below or above a chord tone. In bluegrass we only emphasize the neighbor tones which come from below using the following formula: neighbor tone → chord tone. Common neighbor tone movements that we already know are the ♭3 → 3rd movement and the M7 → Root movement. The last neighbor tone movements would be the #4 → 5th movement that is demonstrated in the next example.

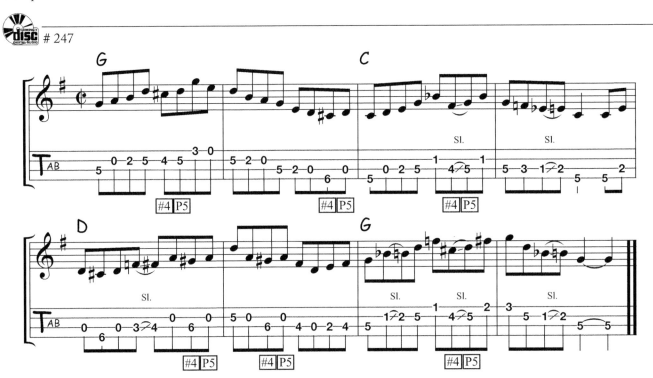

The #4 sliding into the 5th might sound familiar to you, because of the fact that we already played something similar as we combined slides and double-stops in a previous chapter.

Chromatic:

The use of chromatic lines has always been a part of bluegrass music. It can be used as a "spice" in order to give a solo something extra. Exaggerated use of chromatic lines would only work well on a jazzy tune. But what is chromatic? Chromatic is the expression of a line of tones which uses half steps only. Play and listen to the G chromatic scale.

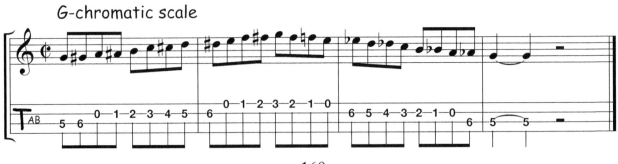

3rd→5th:

The most characteristic and common chromatic line might be the one between the 3rd and the 5th. This chromatic line functions just as well going up as going down. I've written out a couple of examples to play. The last examples make use of some "in between notes" (marked: *) as a variation to plain chromatic playing.

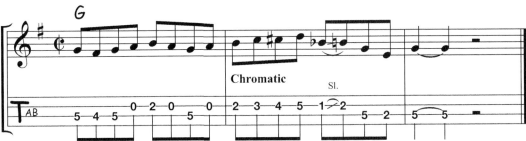

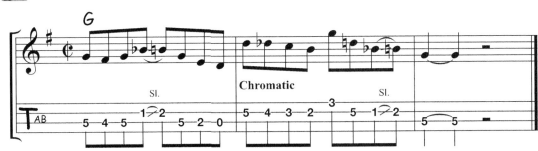

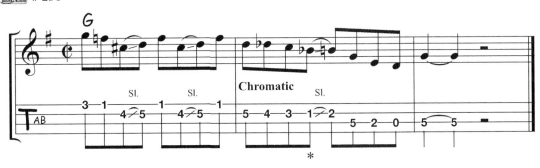

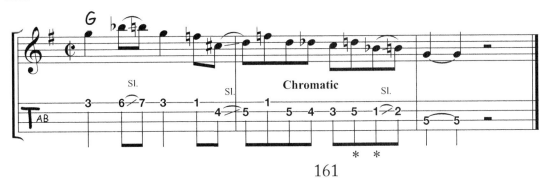

161

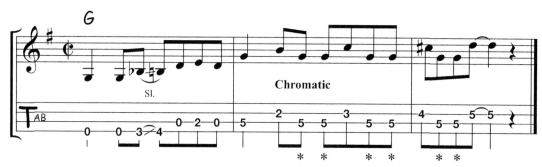

Root → ♭7:

We already touched on the chromatic movement: Root → ♭7 as we learned about the Monroe style (See Chapter 23, page 129). The idea with the Root → ♭7 movement in Monroe style was to emphasize the sound of the ♭7 tone before moving on to the next chord. The Root → ♭7 movement can also appear inside a lick as in the following example:

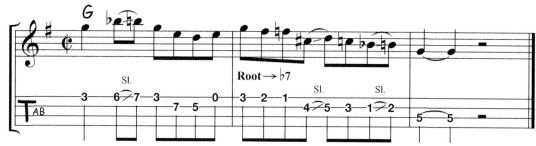

Root → 6th:

Another common chromatic line is the movement from the Root down to the 6th. Actually the Root → 6th movement is just an extension of the Root → ♭7 movement as you can see:

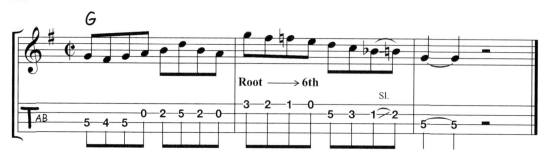

2nd → 3rd:

The three-note movement from the 2nd to the 3rd is also a small chromatic line. It is well known as a part of the legendary guitar G-run:

Mixed chromatic:

The following G lick is a big mixture of all of the different chromatic movements I've talked about. The second lick is based on the plain G chromatic scale. This amount of chromatic might be a little too much for traditional bluegrass, - but you are the "judge," you decide.

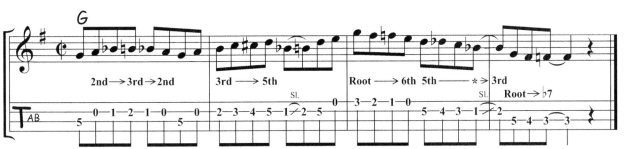

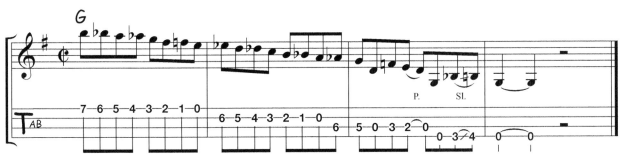

The minor pentatonic scale:

The minor pentatonic scale is like the major pentatonic scale, a scale made out of five tones (penta = five). The minor pentatonic scale is based on the minor scale. You just have to leave out the 2nd and 6th of the minor scale in order to get the minor pentatonic scale.

163

A-minor scale

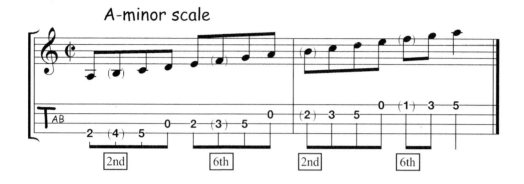

A-minor pentatonic scale

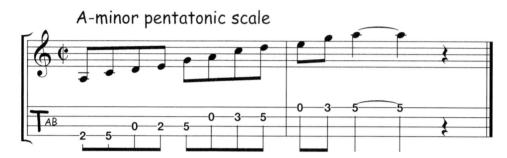

Now try to compare the minor pentatonic scale to the blues scale. As you can see, the blues scale is based on the minor pentatonic scale.

A-blues scale

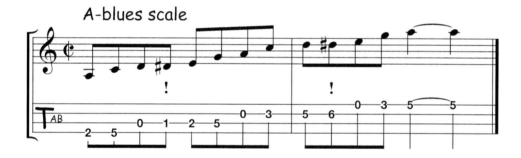

In practice, the minor pentatonic scale could be used as a substitute for the blues scale. It would certainly work out very well, but it won't have as strong of a bluesy sound as the blues scale.

Mountain minor tunes:

As we learned about the mountain minor sound (Chapter 22 – The Blues Scale), I taught you about the use of the blues scale as a foundation for horizontal improvising. If you don't like the bluesy sound in a mountain minor tune, the minor pentatonic scale would be your choice (see "Pretty Polly" – Chapter 25). Also the minor (no 6th) and the dorian scale could be used on mountain minor tunes (see Chapter 20). It's all about the sound– and what you prefer.

Minor chords:

Could the minor pentatonic scale also be used with minor chords appearing in a major key tune? It would be a lie to say no, but I actually prefer the minor (no 6th) scale for improvising with minor chords (or the minor/dorian scales– see Chapter 20). To me, the minor pentatonic scale doesn't sound that melodic because of the missing 2nd scale tone. If you listen to the following two examples you'll get my point.

164

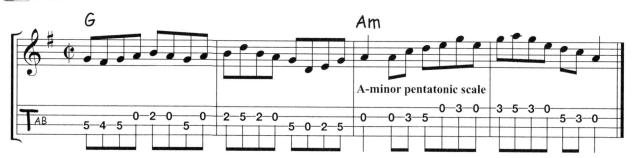

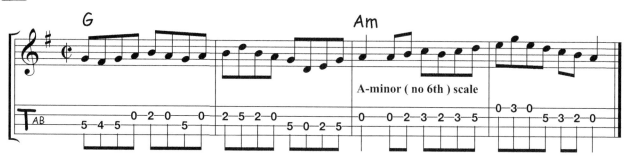

The relative minor:

This often-used chord movement makes use of the following formula: "Major chord $\rightarrow$ Minor chord" (played 1½ step lower). The most common ones in bluegrass music are:

G → Em	C → Am	A → F♯m	D → Bm
F → Dm	B♭ → Gm	E → C♯m	B → G♯m

If we compare for example, the tone material of the G and the Em chords, we'll see that two out of three tones are the same:

G = **g b** d   Em = e **g b**   Em7 = e **g b d**

We'll also find a similar relationship between the G-major scale and the E-minor scale, as well as between the G-major pentatonic scale and the E-minor pentatonic scale:

G-major scale

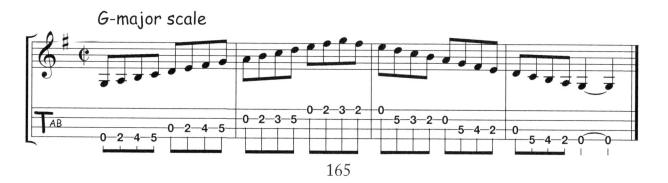

E-minor scale

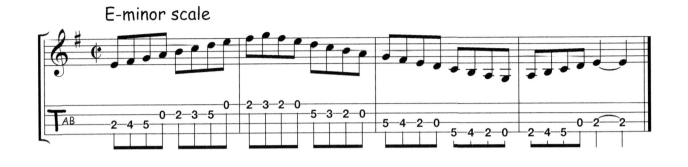

G-major pentatonic scale

E-minor pentatonic scale

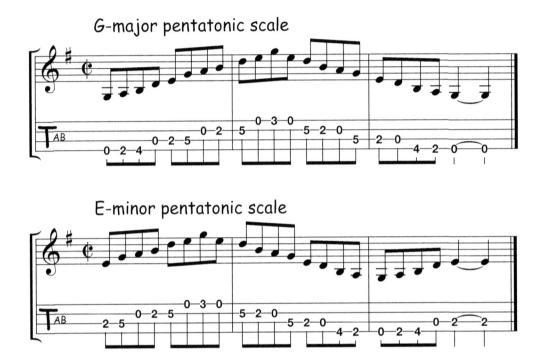

Because of this relationship, we also say, for example, that E-minor is the **relative** minor to G-major, and visa versa. You'll also find the same chord tone/scale relationship by all of the other "major → minor chord" movements that I've already listed. It means: A-minor is the relative minor to C-major, F♯-minor is the relative minor to A-major, B-minor is the relative minor to D-major, etc.

A substitution:

Quite often the minor chord in a "major chord → relative minor chord" movement comes as a replacement/substitution for the major chord. In order to understand the idea, I've made a couple of examples to play. **A "major chord → relative minor chord" substitution only works if the minor chord fits the melody of the played tune.** Notice that the Am and the Bm chord don't come as part of a "major chord → relative minor chord" movement, but just as a substitution for the "original" major chord.

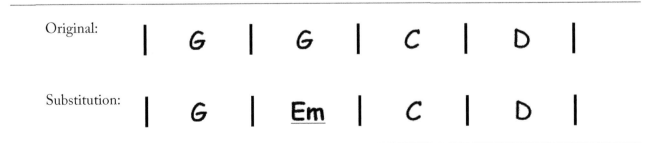

166

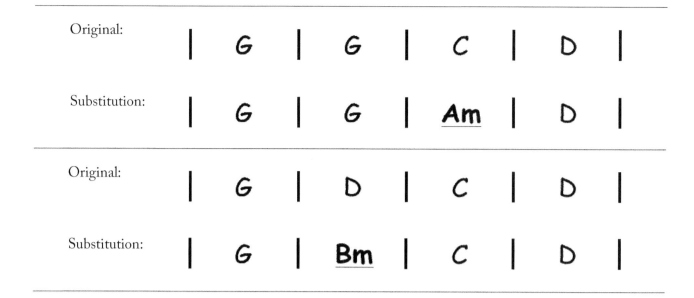

Where or how to use the relative minor chords is really up to you (and your fellow musicians).

Improvising using substitution:

Because of the relationship between our "relative chords," it's obvious that this know-how can be used in improvising too. A common case is the following situation: You and a friend are playing a tune and you're improvising. He makes an unexpected move to a relative minor chord, while you're still improvising over the major chord. – Does this work? Yes, it might actually work out very well as demonstrated in the next example.

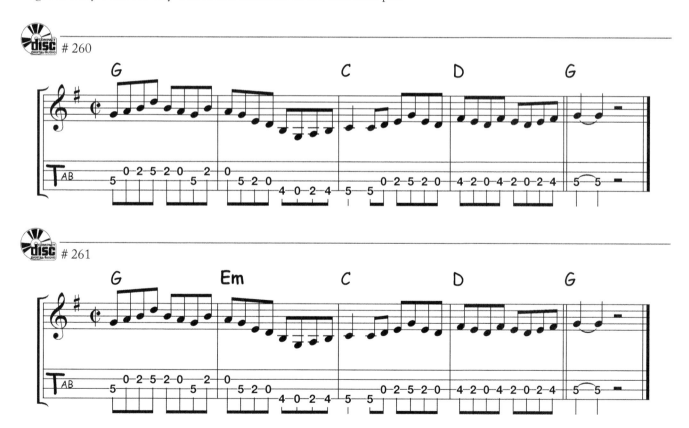

The above example was based on the pentatonic scales. The scale played with the Em chord was thought of as a G-major pentatonic scale, which actually contains the same tones as the E-minor pentatonic scale.

167

Ok, it worked but what about the other way around? Does an Em lick also fit with the G chord? Yes, it might also work, but I wouldn't start on an Em lick using the root as the first tone, because of the fact that the e tone doesn't belong to the G chord tones. But let's try to use an Em lick (starting on the root) on the second G chord bar to see if it would work.

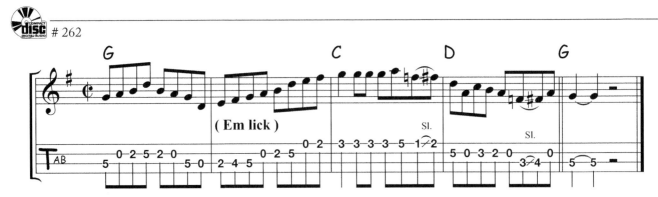

It wasn't perfect, but it was usable. If we start our Em lick on a different chord tone than the root, an Em lick would become perfect on the G chord too.

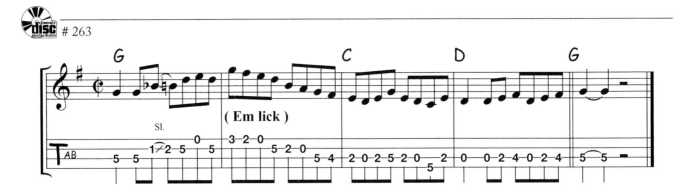

Where and how to use substitutions:

I think the best place to use substitution is in the situation where the accompanists change to a relative minor chord, but we want to keep on playing over the major chord. Check out the next solo, in which the improvisation is based on the major chords only.

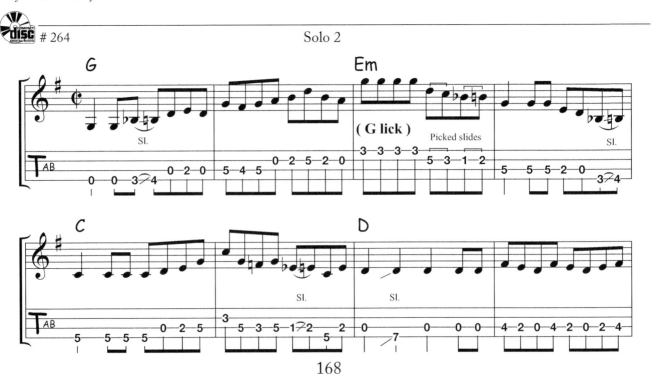

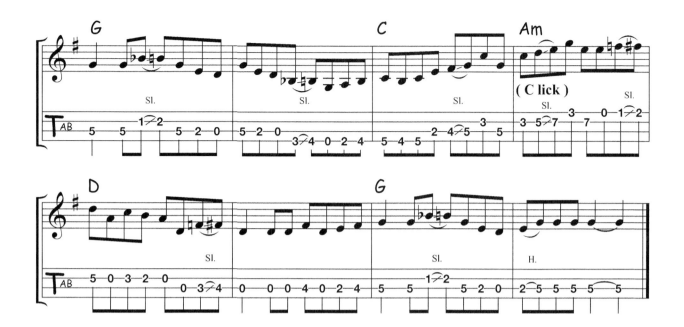

Another situation where a substitution could work out very well would be on a tune in which a minor chord appears, for which we don't have any licks. For example, do you have one or more C♯m licks? – No! Me neither, but I do have a bunch of E licks and E is the relative major to C♯m. Let's play an example.

265

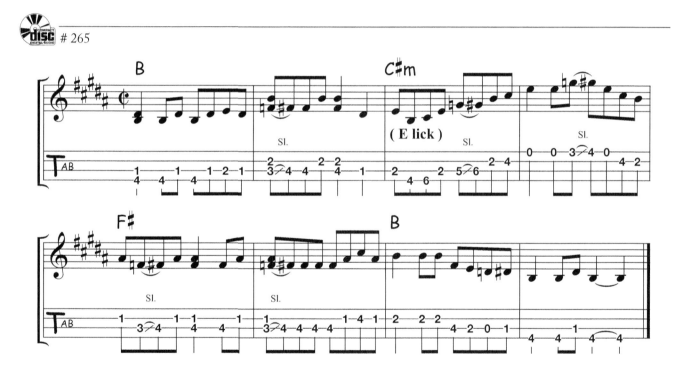

NOTICE: The use of a major chord-based improvisation as a substitute for the relative minor chord, only sounds good if we try to avoid the use of the ♭7 "spice." The flatted seventh of the G chord would be the tone f, which doesn't fit the relative minor chord (the Em chord).

ASSIGNMENTS

If you made it so far as to understand the material in this chapter, you did a really good job. Try to come out with a couple of your own assignments now. Make them fit your level.

What is a hot lick? To me, a hot lick signifies something special. A hot lick should be a tool to make the listener pay extra attention to what is being played. A hot lick could be used in the beginning of a solo, in order to emphasize the change, but it could also appear inside the solo as a surprise to the listener, or at the very end of the solo as a climax. To me, a hot lick could be described by the following key words: Special, interesting and surprising. Most hot licks are also technically difficult to play, but they don't have to be. A change in sound or rhythm could also create a hot lick.

Instead of coming up with a bunch of hot licks to play, I decided to show you a couple of ideas to use for composing hot licks yourself. The number of ways to play a hot lick is endless, but the following examples will show you at least a couple of ideas to use.

Playing fast:

In order to play something fast on a medium fast tune, we need to use triplets. Triplets are three notes played in the time of one beat. All three notes of a triplet could be picked, but a lot of mandolin players prefer to play them using hammer-on and pull-offs, as done in the following examples.

266

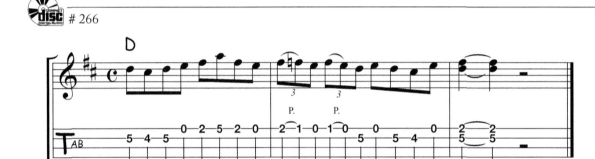

267

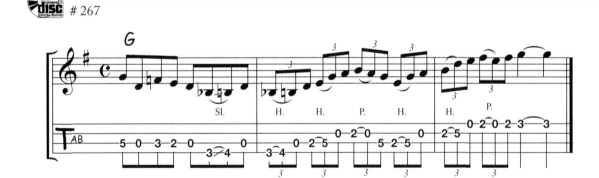

Mixing ideas:

A hot lick could also be made up by mixing all kind of ideas and "spices." To do this, we need to have a good knowledge about scales and theory. It might also take some "trying out" to come up with something useful. The following hot lick is made up of a handful "spices" and even a little blues scale. Try to figure out "what's going on" inside the lick.

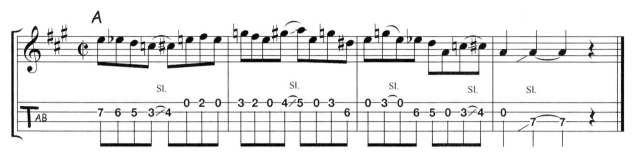

Large movements:

Making an unexpected movement from down the low string to high up on the neck could also come out really surprising. The system also works well the other way around, as you can see in the second example. A thorough knowledge of double-stops up the neck can be a big help when composing "large movement" licks.

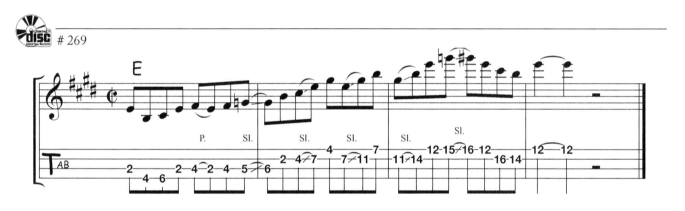

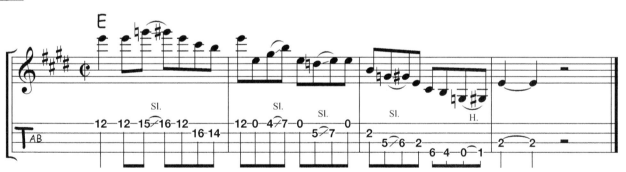

Rhythmic displacement:

Rhythmic displacement is a technique in which the same motif is repeated one or more times. The displacement of the rhythm happens when the repetition starts on an odd beat compared to the original motif. The most common way of rhythmic displacement in bluegrass music is done by repeating a motif of three eighth notes, without making use of rests between the motifs. Notice that depending on how many repetitions we have done, we need to fill out the last bar with one or more "fill out" tones in order to complete the line.

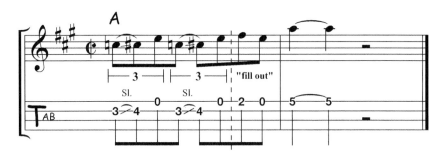

The rhythmic displacement comes out more interesting when the repetition is done more than once. In the following example, the "three-note" motif is repeated throughout two bars of the A chord.

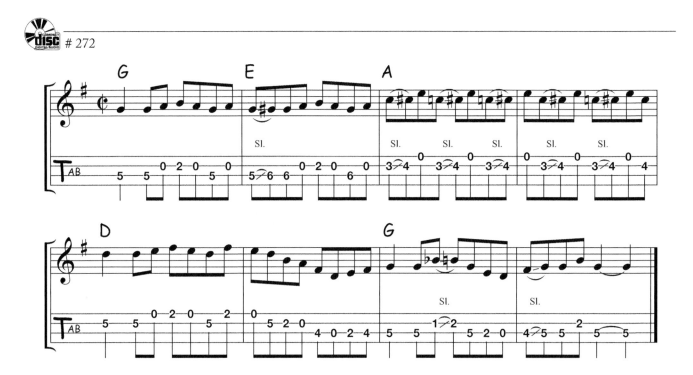

Even more interesting is the use of "six eighth-note" motifs repeated over a couple of bars. The number of ways on which "six-note" motifs could be varied is endless. In the next examples I'll show you a couple of ideas to use.

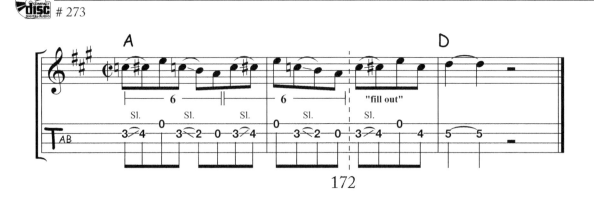

172

274

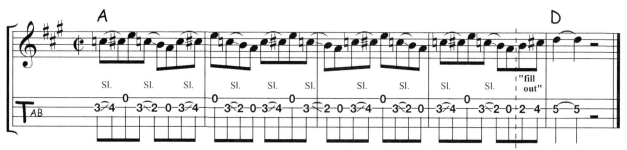

275

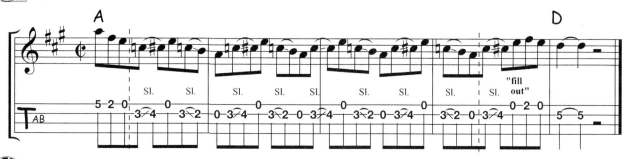

276

277

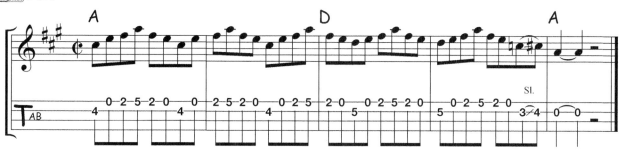

278

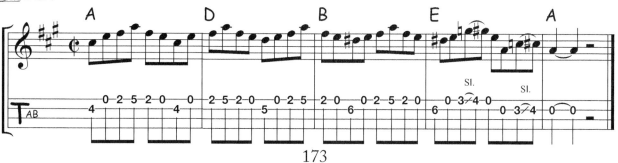

173

As you might have noticed, I've only made use of five tones on the G chord in ex. 276. This kind of variation also works because of the quarter note inside the motif. As long as a motif has the same length as the normal "six-note" motif, we can skip tones or even add some extra tones (triplets or fast sixteen notes).

Using rhythmic displacement spontaneously while improvising might take some practice. The problem is to be able to get back on the track after several measures of rhythmic displaced playing. If you have a couple of composed licks to use, you might be able to vary them after a while.

ASSIGNMENT

1. Come up with some new hot licks using ideas from this chapter.

CHAPTER 28: How to Simplify a Lick

As I started to learn bluegrass music, the biggest problem for me was to be able to play the arrangement of tunes which I found in books and magazines. Quite often the solos had one or more measures which weren't playable to me. Now I had two choices: either practice a lot or simplify the solo. Often I chose the latter solution in order to be able to play the tune at the next jam session. Over the years I've seen people come and go, to whom the only goal was to be able to play some arrangements exactly the same way as their "musical hero." I've even seen musicians stop playing their instruments because they didn't reach their goal. To me, music is all about having fun and to be able to play tunes together with other people in a jam session or even in a band. Of course it's a good idea to practice and learn some difficult licks, but when doing this you need to be able to evaluate yourself and your abilities. If you can't learn the lick in a relatively short period, you might use your time more constructively on something else. Only picking techniques and exercises should normally be practiced over a longer period.

Also, this book might have some parts which aren't that playable to you. Because of the fact that we all learn differently, it might not be the same parts which we all find difficult. As a help to you, I'll demonstrate a couple of ways of how to simplify a lick.

Skipping tones:

The easiest way to simplify a lick is by skipping some of the tones. The fact that many of my examples use a lot of eighth notes might make them difficult to play. If we have a line of four eighth notes, it would nearly always be possible to leave out one or even more of the tones. Before using this system on some licks, I'd like to show you the idea by using it on the fiddle tune "Temperance Reel." Quite often arrangements of fiddle tunes contain a lot of eighth notes as in the following example. The second example is based on the same arrangement, but is much easier to play, because of the "missing tones." An easily-playable arrangement can certainly also be played faster and then we won't miss the "missing tones" so much.

 # 279

Temperance Reel

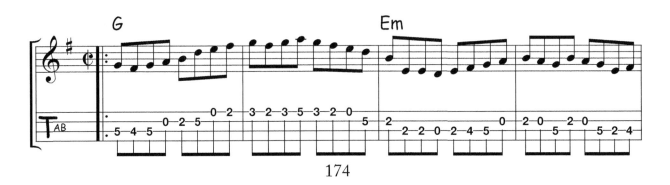

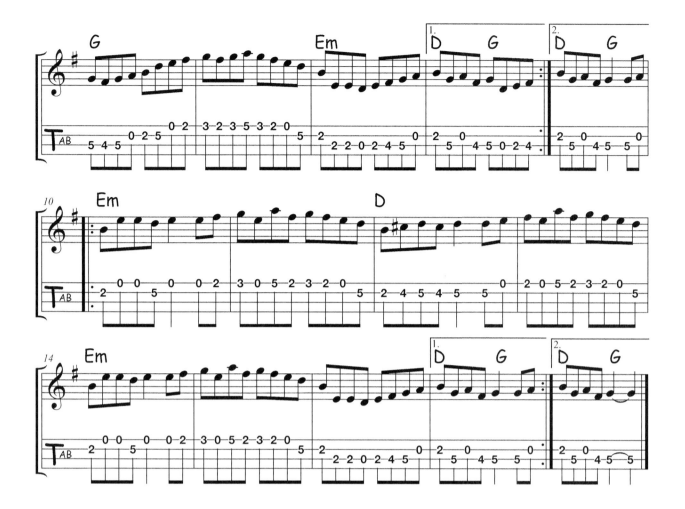

 # 280

Temperance Reel (easy)

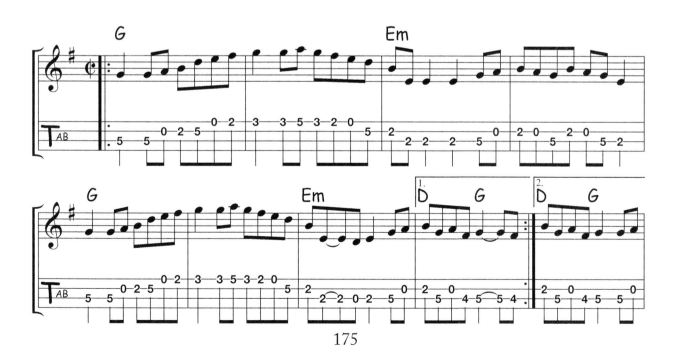

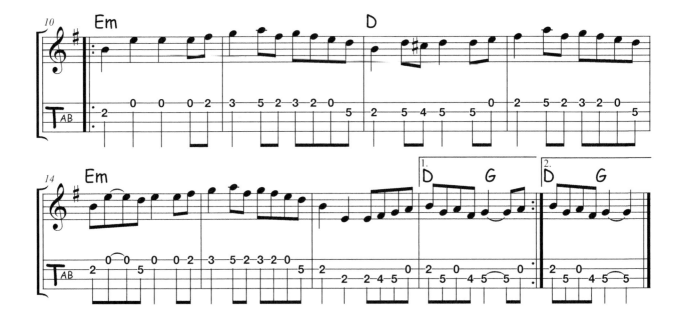

As you can see, it wasn't any problem to simplify the arrangement of "Temperance Reel." Even though the "leaving out tones" system worked out very well this time, we might not be that lucky every time. Sometimes we have to change or move a tone in order to make the system work. I'll give an example: As I made the simplified arrangement of "Temperance Reel," I had this idea to simplify the last bar of the B-part, the one sounding like this:

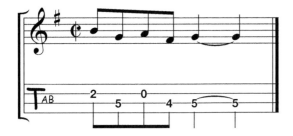

By using the "skipping tones" system I had these three solutions:

Variations 1

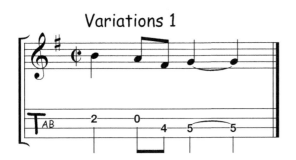

Variations 2

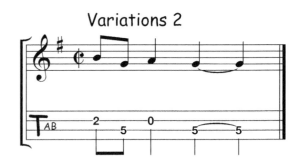

Variations 3

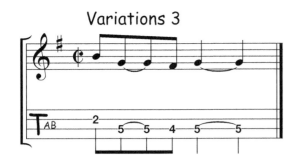

All of the three variations are somewhat usable, but not really perfect. By moving the tones in the first variation a little bit, I started to like the ending, too.

 # 281

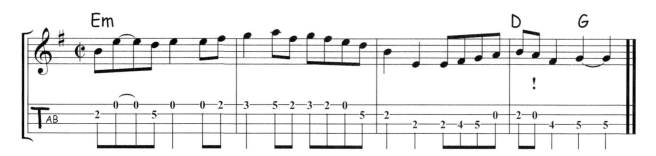

Staying on chord tones:

A lot of the licks in this book are composed with the purpose of demonstrating different scales and their structure. In order to do this, the licks often use many tones moving from the high strings down to the low stings or the other way around.

But actually we don't have to move around that much. The must important tones are the chord tones, and an easy way to simplify a scale-oriented lick is by emphasizing the chord tones instead of moving up and down the scale. Take a look at the following scale-oriented lick and its simplified variation.

 # 282

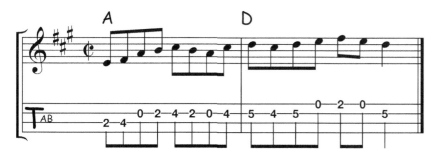

 # 283

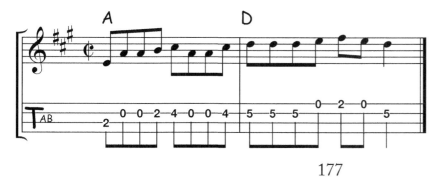

By simplifying a scale-oriented lick using chord tones, we also change the character of the lick. Chord tone-based playing is quite common in bluegrass, especially on fast tunes.

The next solo is a simplified version of solo 2 from Chapter 10. The arrangement is worked out by using the "skipping tones" technique and "chord tone-based playing." Try to compare the two solos and figure out where each technique is used. Notice also that a couple of small tone movements had to be made in order to make it work well.

284

Solo 2 from Chapter 10
(simplified)

Limited improvisation:

Another technique to use when learning to improvise would be the limitation of strings used. Try to learn the arpeggios, the scales and the double-stops on the first and the second string only. Start out with one key - three chords. The next example will show you the system.

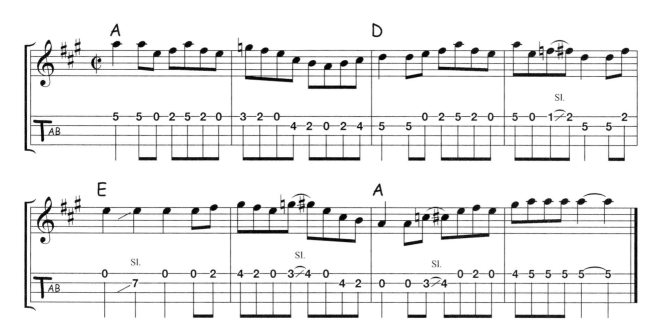

Lick replacement:

A last trick, which I've used a lot, is the replacement of difficult licks. The replacement technique is a good alternative to the simplification techniques we've just learned. The idea is to skip a whole lick and to replace it with something totally different within the harmonic structure. As an example, I've written out a small line in which a tricky cross picking lick is used. In the second example I've replaced the cross picking lick with something more playable.

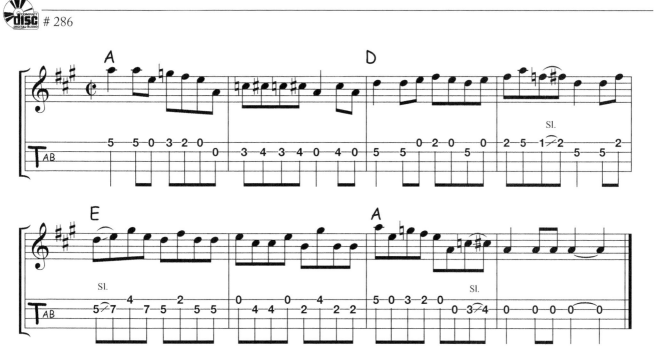

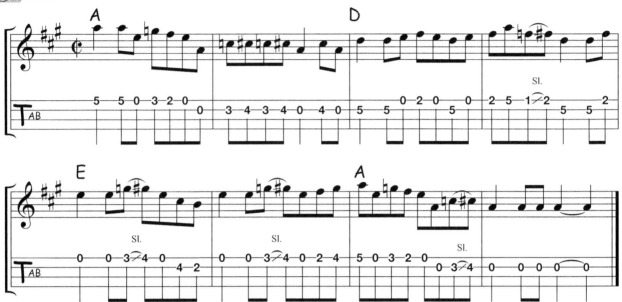

To me, the use of simplified/replaced licks, has opened up some doors in the past, which made me able to play the tunes I'd like to jam or use in a band. You shouldn't hesitate to simplify a difficult lick or solo either. Even really good players use simplified licks when a solo break has to be played in a song in a difficult key like B-major. All of you who have tried to play a major pentatonic lick with an F# chord (see Chapter 16) know how difficult it is. Why not play something simplified? I would!

ASSIGNMENTS

1. The first thing to do would be to simplify a lick in which a lot of eighth notes are used.

2. Try to use the simplification techniques on a fiddle tune.

3. If you feel comfortable with the system, then use it on a more difficult solo. If some of the licks get too difficult to simplify, then utilize the replacement technique. Make it easy and playable!

CONCLUSION

Learning to improvise can be compared to the process of learning a foreign language. When learning a language, we need to know something about grammar, but we also have to build up a vocabulary to use in conversations. In music, the theory could be compared to the grammar we have in a language and our "bag of licks" to the vocabulary. When we are learning to improvise, a lot of things have to be trained the same way as when learning a new language. Slow improvisation is like writing a letter, taking the time it takes to check out the right spelling and word order in order to come up with a perfect result. When we have to make conversation in another language, it's important to have a certain vocabulary, but we also have to be able to put the words together in understandable sentences. When improvising we also need to have a certain amount of licks/ideas to use in building lines, but we also have to be able to make a smooth transition between the licks/ideas. With conversational training we might start out to learn how to make a room-reservation in a hotel or how to order in a restaurant. It would be nonsense to begin learning how to make a business conversation before knowing some daily life conversation, just as it would be nonsense to begin learning improvising in the key of B♭ or even D♭, before knowing how to treat A-major.

When comparing the learning process of a foreign language to that of improvisation, it might be easier to understand the importance of a step-by-step learning procedure. You can read a lot, but if you don't try to put the theory into practice, you won't be able to use it. The great thing about improvisation (or learning a language) is that we don't have to learn/know everything in order to start out using it in practice. The first "sentences" might come out shaky, but each time it gets better and better. – I promise you!

APPENDIX

Content:

How to read the box system . . . . page 181

Major arpeggios . . . . page 182

Minor arpeggios . . . . page 183

Major scales . . . . page 184

Major pentatonic scales. page 186

Minor pentatonic scales . . . . page 188

Blues scales . . . . page 190

Minor scales . . . . page 192

Minor (no 6th) scales . . . . page 194

Harmonic minor scales. . . . . page 196

Harmonic minor (no 6th) scales . . . . page 198

Chord progressions. . . . . page 200

How to read the box system:

The most important thing about understanding the box system is not to see the illustrated fingerboard as a reflection of your own mandolin as when looking in a mirror. The box system is actually constructed the same way as the tablature system, which means that the lower line depicts the G string(s) and the high one the E string(s).

Fingerboard:

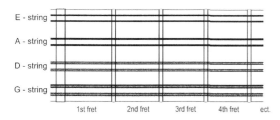

Box system:

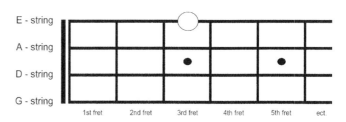

The circle on the E string indicates a fretted note played on the E string 3rd fret (the tone G). A circle behind the double-line (the nut) would symbolize an open string. The black spots on the neck are the dot inlays (be aware of a possible difference in the dot inlay patterns on your mandolin).

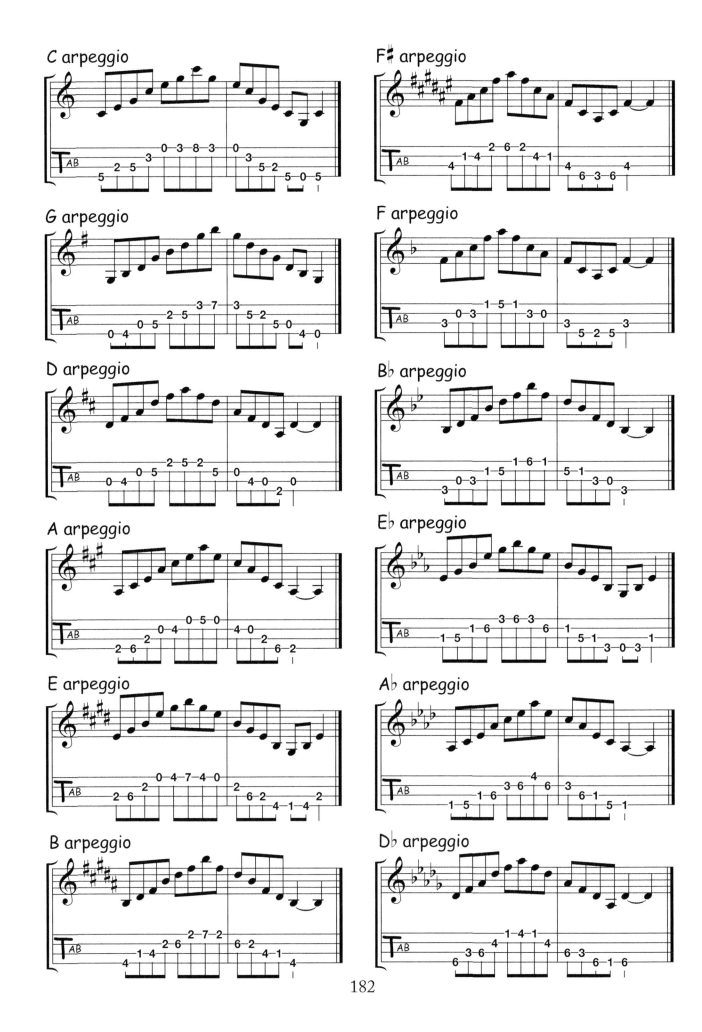

182

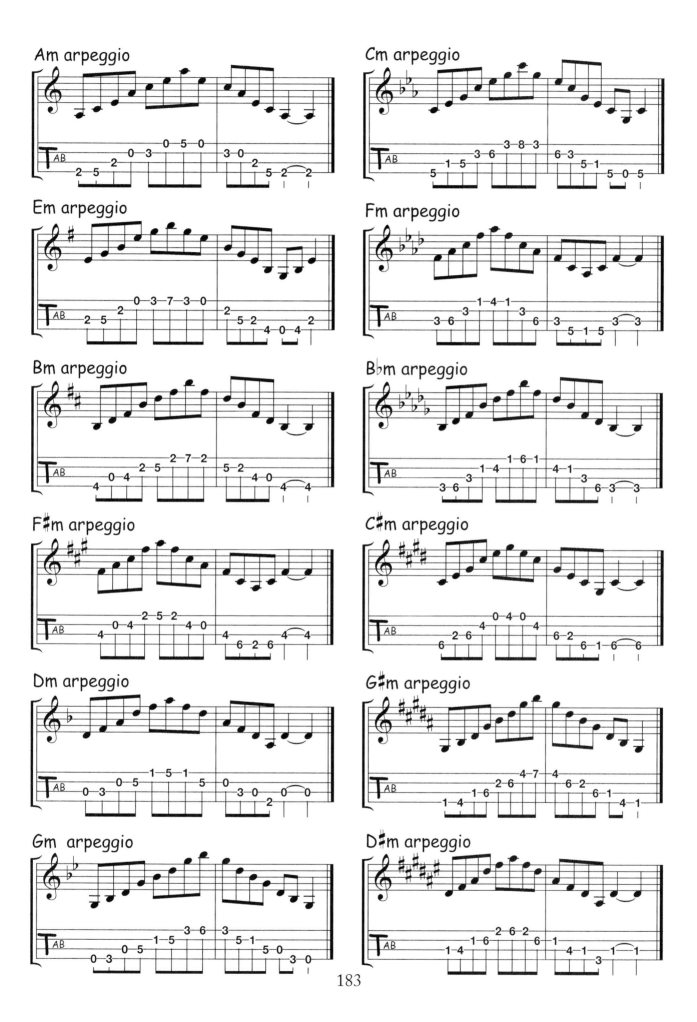

183

Major scales

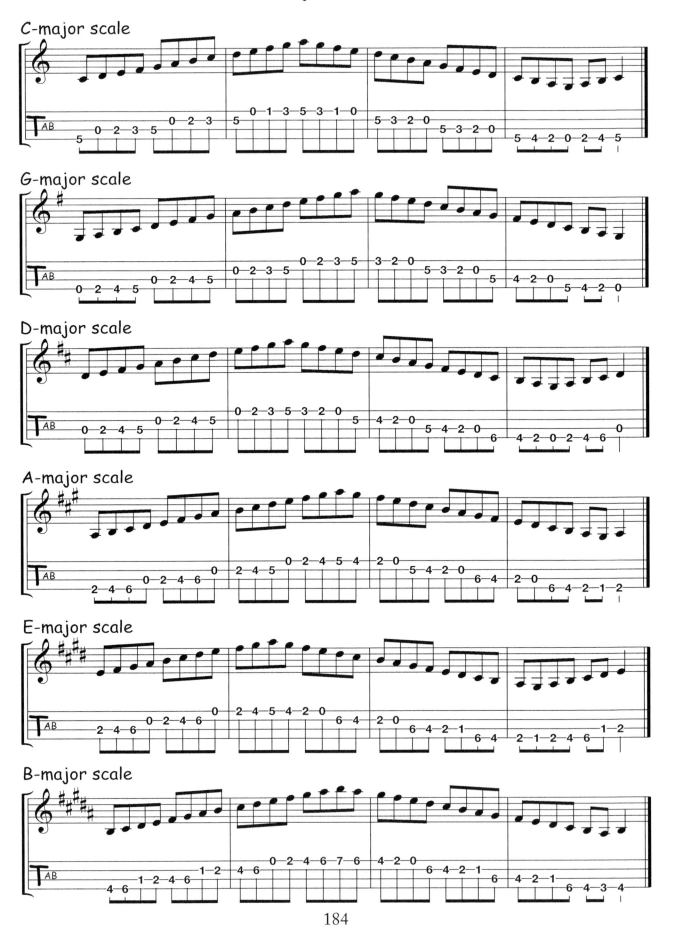

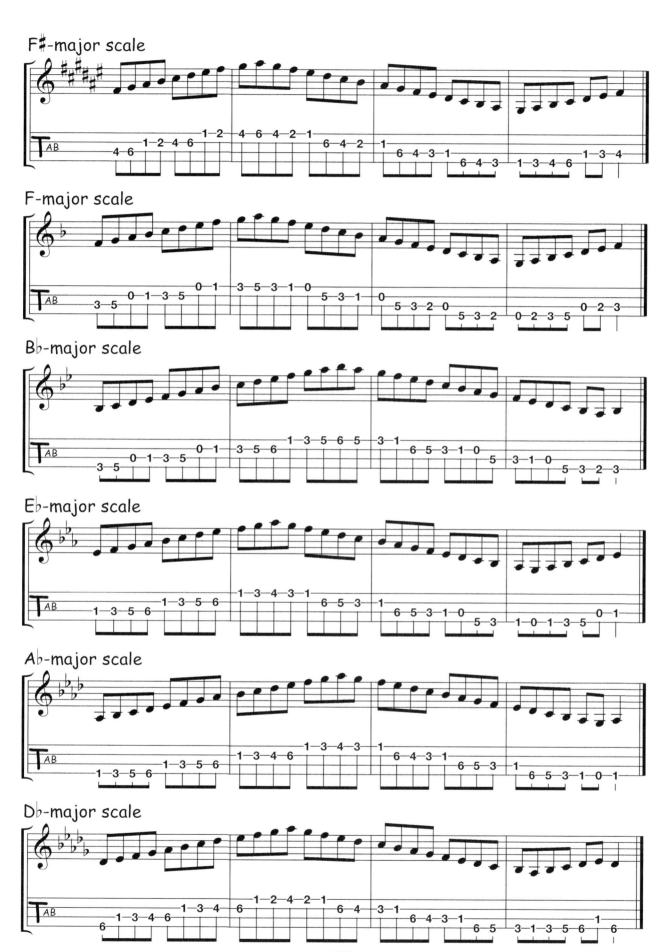

F#-major scale

F-major scale

Bb-major scale

Eb-major scale

Ab-major scale

Db-major scale

Major pentatonic scales

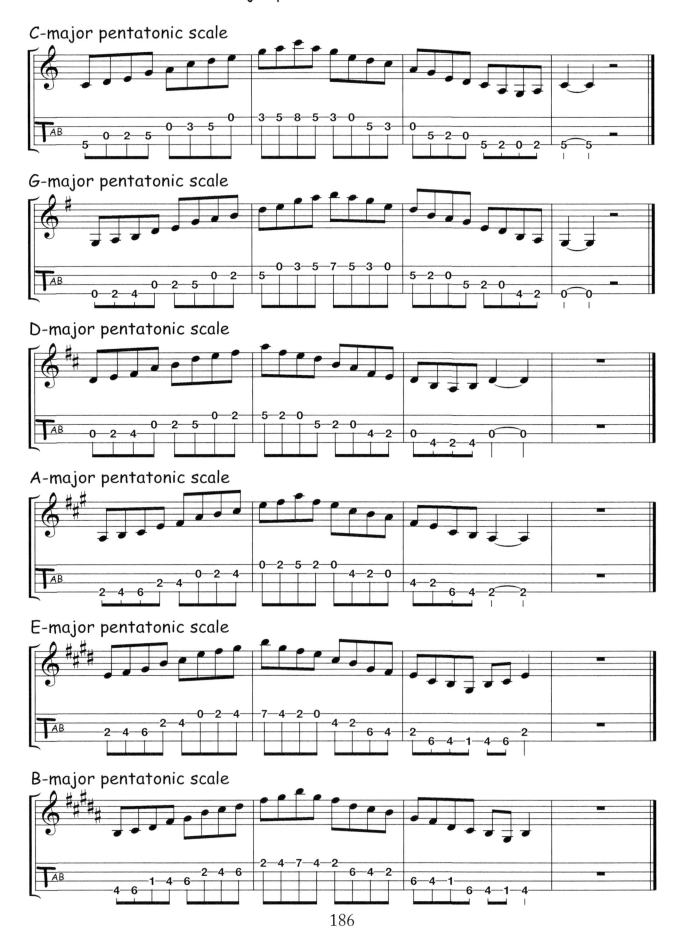

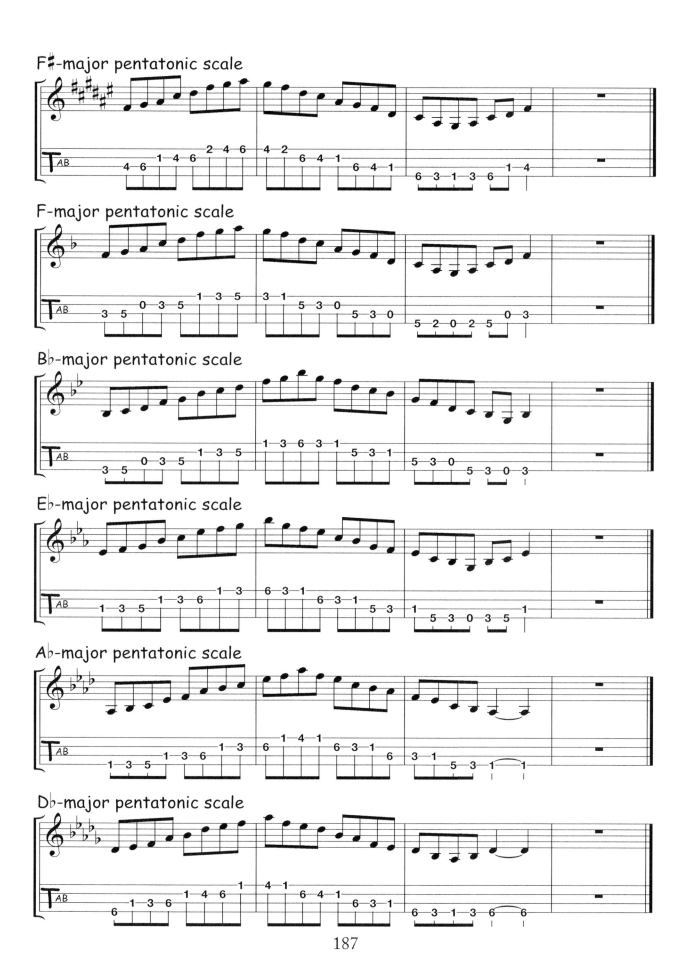

187

Minor pentatonic scales

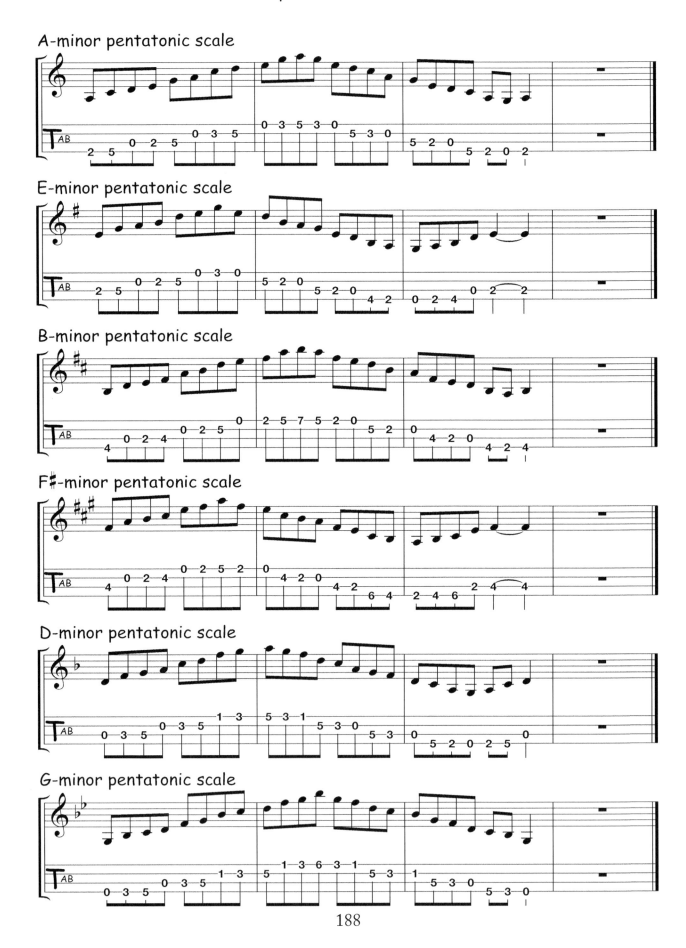

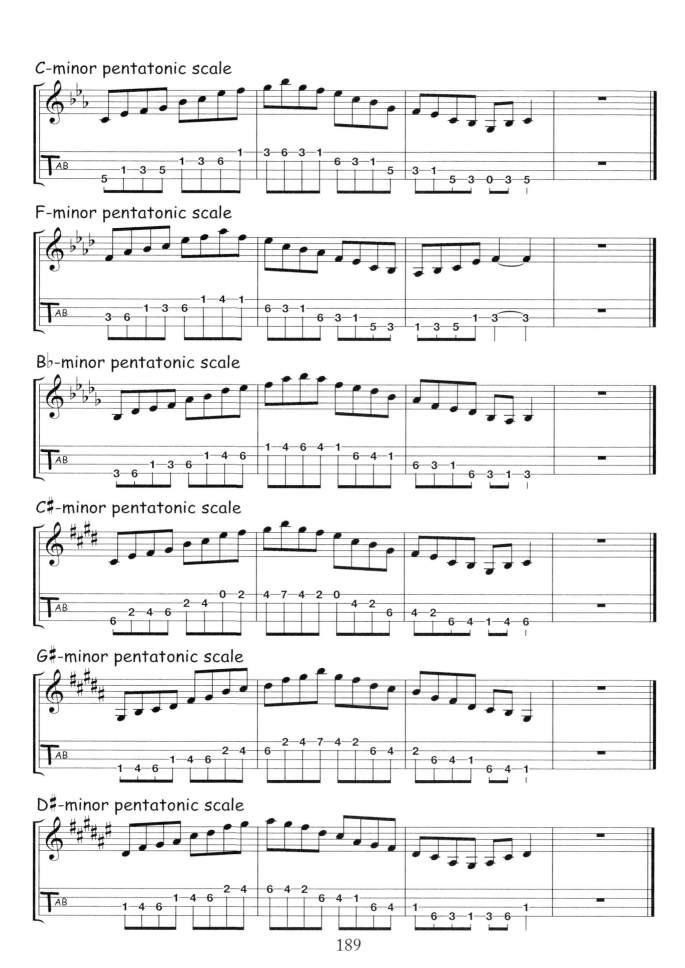

189

Blues scales

A blues scale

E blues scale

B blues scale

F# blues scale

D blues scale

G blues scale

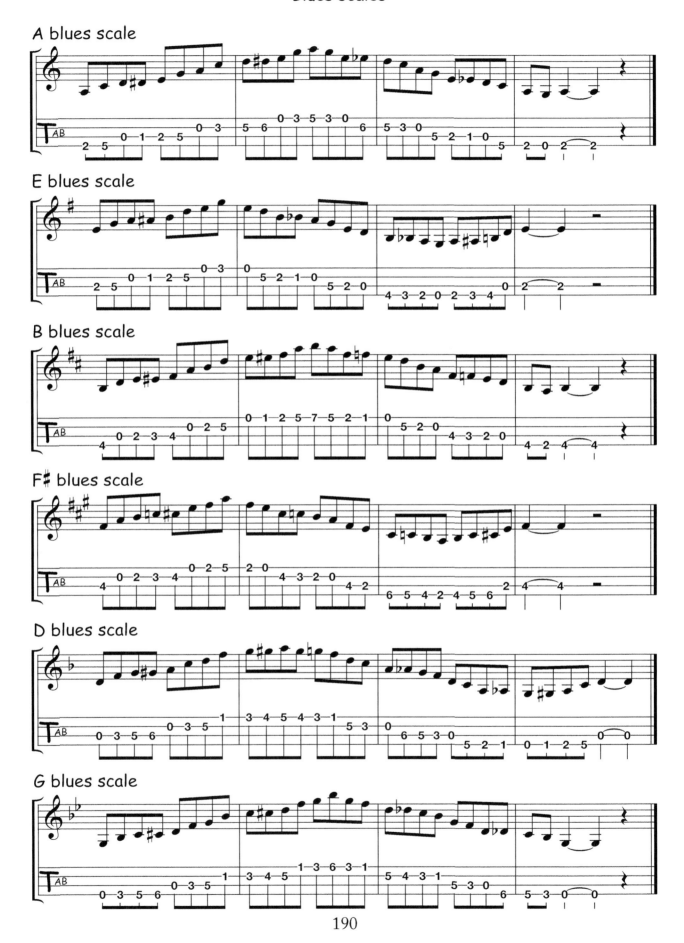

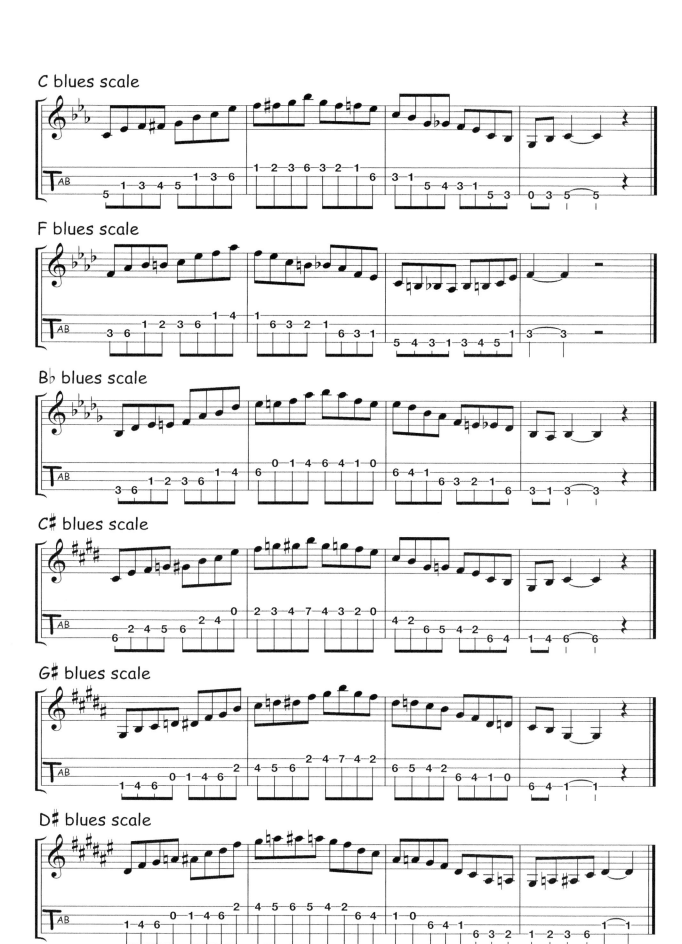

Minor scales

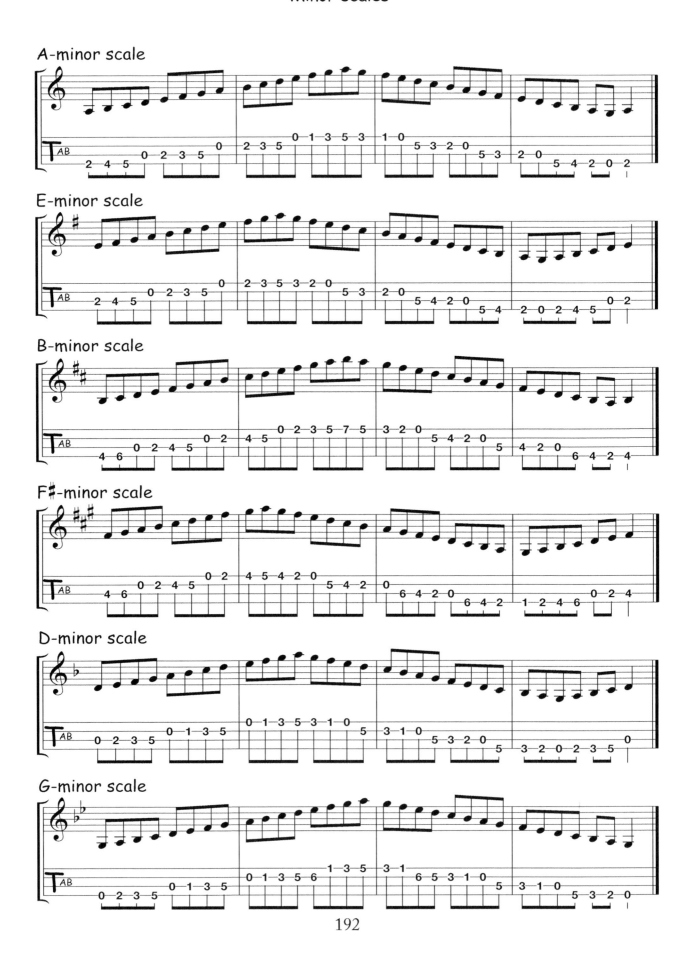

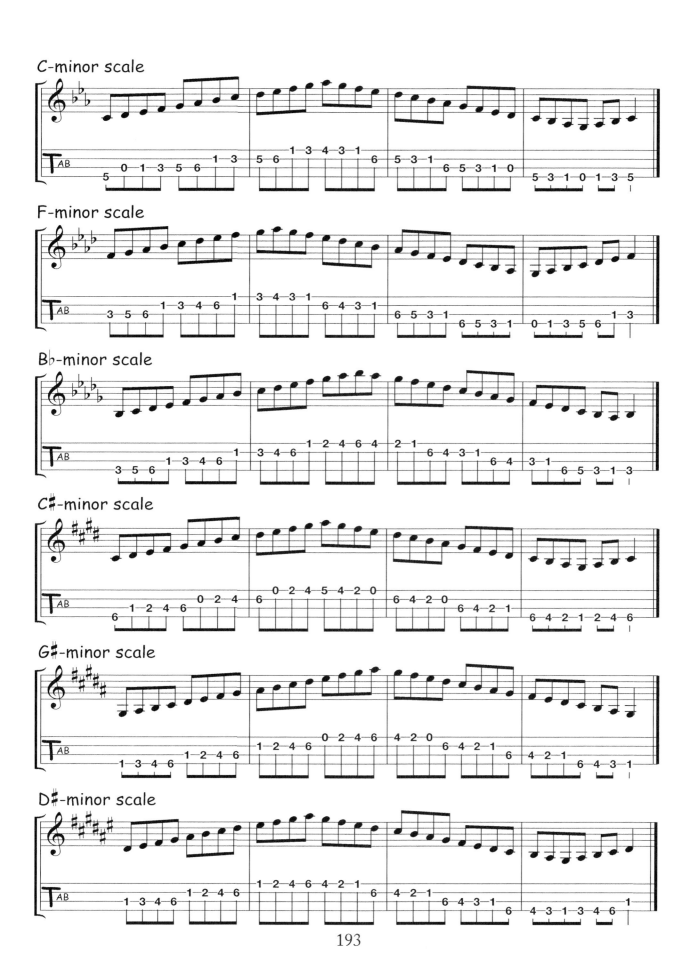

Minor (no 6th) scales

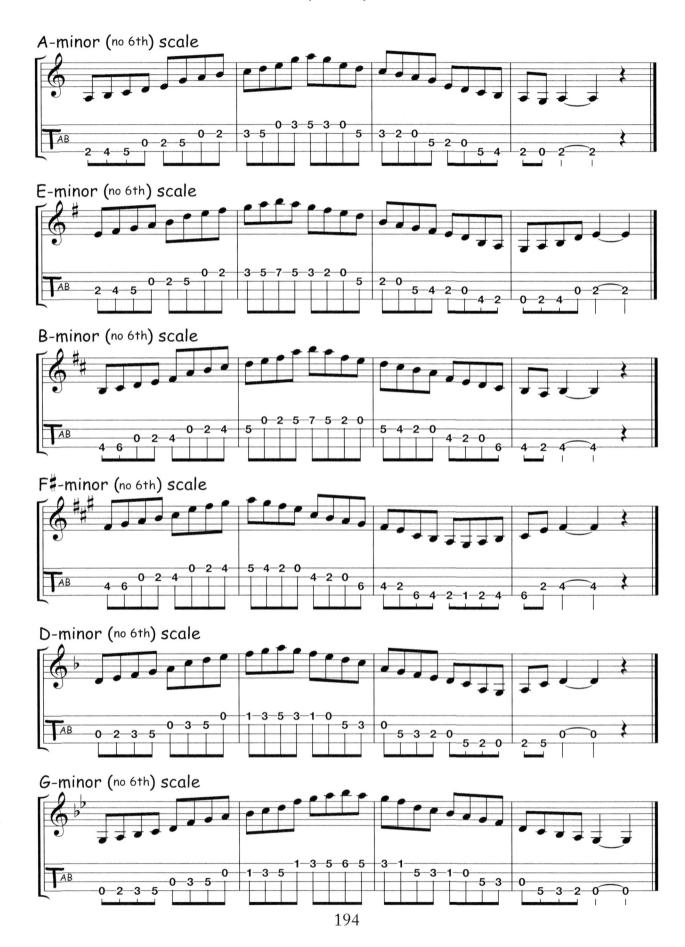

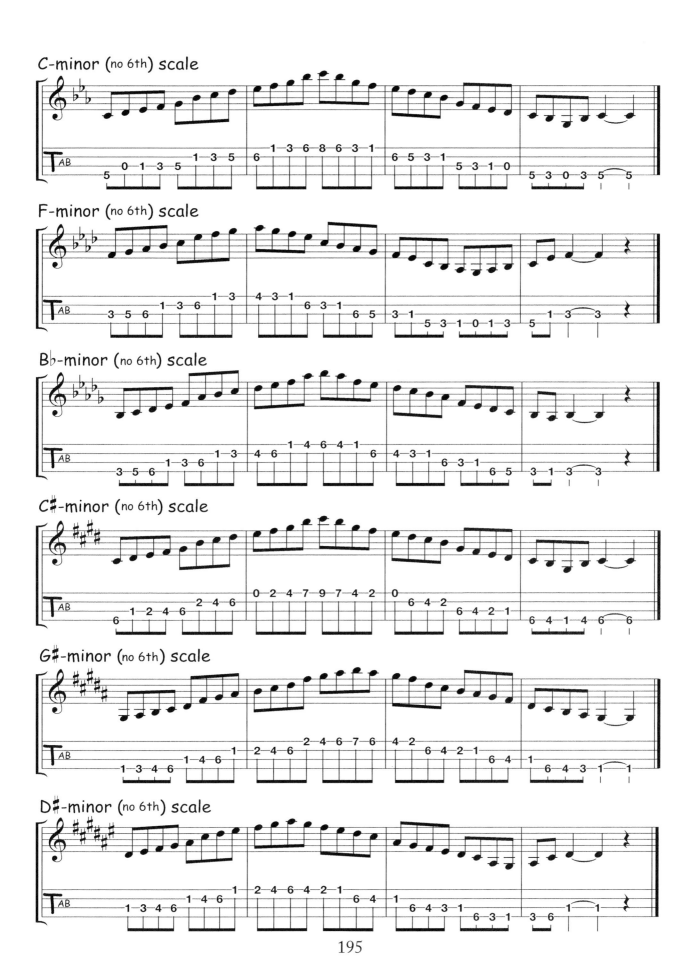
195

Harmonic minor scales

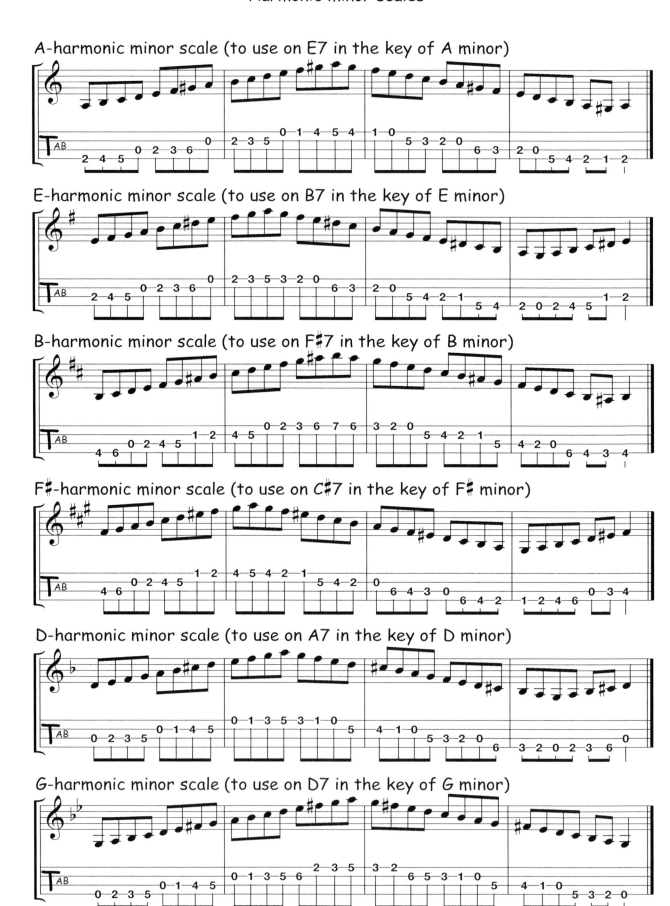

A-harmonic minor scale (to use on E7 in the key of A minor)

E-harmonic minor scale (to use on B7 in the key of E minor)

B-harmonic minor scale (to use on F#7 in the key of B minor)

F#-harmonic minor scale (to use on C#7 in the key of F# minor)

D-harmonic minor scale (to use on A7 in the key of D minor)

G-harmonic minor scale (to use on D7 in the key of G minor)

C-harmonic minor scale (to use on G7 in the key of C minor)

F-harmonic minor scale (to use on C7 in the key of F minor)

Bb-harmonic minor scale (to use on F7 in the key of Bb minor)

C#-harmonic minor scale (to use on G#7 in the key of C# minor)

G#-harmonic minor scale (to use on D#7 in the key of G# minor)

D#-harmonic minor scale (to use on A#7 in the key of D# minor)

197

Harmonic minor (no 6th) scales

C-harmonic minor (no 6th) scale   (to use on G7 in the key of C minor)

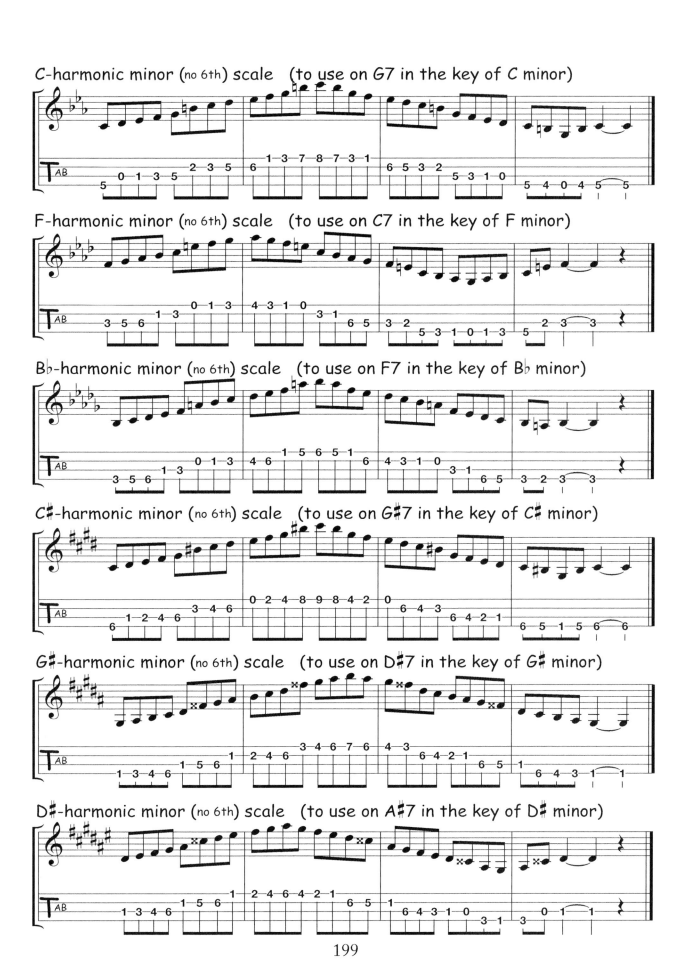

F-harmonic minor (no 6th) scale   (to use on C7 in the key of F minor)

B♭-harmonic minor (no 6th) scale   (to use on F7 in the key of B♭ minor)

C♯-harmonic minor (no 6th) scale   (to use on G♯7 in the key of C♯ minor)

G♯-harmonic minor (no 6th) scale   (to use on D♯7 in the key of G♯ minor)

D♯-harmonic minor (no 6th) scale   (to use on A♯7 in the key of D♯ minor)

199

Chord progression #1

‖ A | A | D | D |
| E | E | A | A |
| A | A | D | D |
| E | E | A | A ‖

Chord progression #2

‖ A | A | A | A |
| D | D | A | A |
| D | D | A | A |
| E | E | A | A ‖

Chord progression #3

‖ A | A | D | D |
| A | A | E | E |
| A | A | D | D |
| A | E | A | A ‖

Chord progression #4

‖ A | A | A | A |
| A | A | E | E |
| A | A | D | D |
| A | E | A | A ‖

Chord progression #5

‖ A | A | D | A |
| A | A | E | E |
| A | A | D | A |
| A | E | A | A ‖

Printed in Great Britain
by Amazon

11380599R00115